THE GREATEST MYSTERY IN THE WORLD

Og Mandino

FAWCETT CREST • NEW YORK

A Fawcett Crest Book
Published by The Ballantine Publishing Group
Copyright © 1997 by Elizabeth L. Mandino

http://www.randomhouse.com

Library of Congress Catalog Card Number: 97-97150

ISBN 0-449-22503-8

Manufactured in the United States of America

First Hardcover Edition: April 1997
First Mass Market Edition: April 1998

10   9

For my grandson . . .

BENNETT LEWIS MANDINO

With love . . .

Compared to what we ought to be, we are only half awake. Our fires are dampened, our drafts are checked, and we are making use of only a small part of our mental and physical resources.

—*William James*

THE GREATEST MYSTERY IN THE WORLD

I

$\mathscr{M}$emories. I can still hear his gentle but deep voice saying the words as if they had been spoken just this morning instead of so very long ago.

"How our earth was created and hangs suspended in space or how our minds and bodies repeatedly perform their daily miraculous functions is most difficult to comprehend but the greatest mystery still confronting mankind is that despite all the tools that God provided, both mental and physical, so much of humanity continues to stumble along the rocky paths of failure and sorrow, poverty, and despair."

More than twenty years have passed since I

first heard that wise declaration and yet I am certain that the sentence, despite its length, is being quoted to you verbatim. It was spoken by a wise old man, Simon Potter, whom I first met one snowy morning in the parking lot behind the building in north Chicago that housed the magazine I headed, *Success Unlimited*. He was feeding pigeons from a large brown paper bag as I slowly pulled into the lot and our initial brief greeting that morning was the beginning of a relationship that has affected my entire life.

Following that first meeting, in the mid-seventies, Simon and I soon became close friends. Very often, after a long and pressure-packed day of trying to run a national publication, with all of its challenges, I would walk wearily through the dingy parking lot, enter the old stone building across the street, climb the stairway to his second-story apartment, number 21, and visit with the old man before the long drive to my suburban home. His wise advice and counsel, always served with a glass of white sherry, often helped me to relax and see my problems in a more rational light, and I'm certain that his loving thoughts and wisdom have often been reflected in my work and how I've tried to deal with the world since those memorable days, long ago.

Simon's tiny three-room apartment, clean and dust-free, had one distinguishing feature. Books! Books everywhere, not only crammed into several huge wooden bookcases but also piled tall and neat in columns against every available wall. The old gentleman proudly explained that they were his lifetime collection of "hand of God" books and in response to my puzzled expression he said that he truly believed that certain books were written with God's hand resting lightly upon the author's so that the words inscribed on paper or parchment were being presented directly to us containing God's principles, guidelines, and wise advice on how to lead a better life.

I am six feet tall but Simon was at least a head taller and although he was seventy-eight years old he also told me he was still a working man ... self-employed as a "human ragpicker." He said that he spent most of his days and nights searching out people who had made a failure of their lives and found themselves on humanity's junk pile of misery and despair. Whenever he discovered such lost souls, and they were everywhere, he exclaimed, he would use his "hand of God" books to teach them how to regain their hope and self-esteem.

When Simon learned that I was not only an

editor but had been fortunate enough to publish several books including a bestseller, *The Greatest Salesman in the World*, he told me that he had been working for years on writing a simple piece which contained short but powerful rules of life necessary for one's success. He admitted that he had used many of his "hand of God" books as his reference source and so he had been considering calling his finished work "A Memorandum from God." He even dropped hints, during several of my visits, that perhaps I might consider using his small piece in one of my future books so that it would be read by far greater numbers than he could ever possibly reach.

As our friendship strengthened during the summer and fall of 1974, Simon began addressing me as "Mister Og." In long discussions, where I did far more listening than talking, we covered a wide range of subjects from the benefits of good self-help books to the sorry state of our world. It was, by far, the most memorable time of my life and yet, for reasons I still do not understand, I never mentioned my relationship with Simon to anyone at the office nor did I ever say anything to my wife, Bette, about this giant who was gradually teaching me how to live a more fulfilling life.

Then, on a Monday morning I shall never forget, my world suddenly shifted. I had been away from the magazine for several weeks, promoting *The Greatest Salesman in the World* on a nationwide tour, and I arrived at my office very early in order to tackle the expected backlog of challenges. On my desk was a large brown envelope, addressed to me, with its postage stamps still uncanceled. Upon reading the words "from an old ragpicker" in the upper left-hand corner, I immediately dropped the package and raced out of the office. When I reached the parking lot I dashed between cars, crossed the street, and entered Simon's old apartment building. I hurried up the stairs, ran down the hallway to his apartment, and began pounding on his door. Finally it was opened by a plump woman in a dingy robe with a small child in her arms. When I asked for Simon Potter she began closing the door. She said she didn't know any Simon Potter and in the four years she had lived in the apartment she had never seen the man I described to her.

I didn't know what to say or think. Finally she slammed the door in my face and I retreated slowly down the stairs. In the lobby I turned to a downward stairway and, luckily, found the building's janitor sitting next to the furnace reading a newspaper. He said he had worked there for eleven years and had never seen anyone answering to my description of Simon. In the next several hours of anguish I checked with the police station on Foster Avenue, Cook County Hospital, Missing Persons, and even the county morgue on West Polk. None had any record of a person fitting Simon's description. With a heavy pain in my chest I finally returned to my office and closed the door. I slowly opened the large brown envelope and read Simon's message to me. Enclosed, he wrote, was "The God Memorandum." He asked that I apply its wisdom to my own life for a hundred days and if it worked for me perhaps I might consider sharing it with the world in one of my books. I was not to worry about him. He was embarking on a special mission and although we would not see each other for a long time he wanted me to know that he loved me and would pray for me. I sat staring down at my hands for the longest time after finishing his letter. Then I picked up "The God Memorandum" and read it slowly. It was everything I expected and more and, like Simon's spoken words to me, it became a map by which I have tried to navigate my life, even to this day.

Not until several months after Simon's mysterious disappearance did I finally tell everything to

Bette one evening as we were preparing for bed. She sat close to me, on my side of the bed, and listened intently for more than an hour, without interrupting, as I related all I could remember about my experiences with the old ragpicker.

Finally she grasped my hand firmly and asked, "In your search for him, did anyone . . . anyone . . . admit to ever seeing this man? Anyone in your office? Anyone in the neighborhood?"

I shook my head. "No one. It's as if he never existed except for me."

Bette kissed my cheek, rose, walked around me, and removed an old dictionary from the bookcase against the wall. She turned several pages before pausing and looking toward me before she began reading, "Angel . . . a spiritual being superior to man in power and intelligence . . . an attendant and messenger of God . . . any representative of God, as a prophet or teacher."

She replaced the book, walked slowly around to her side of the bed, pulled back the covers and said softly, "Good night, darling."

In my next book, *The Greatest Miracle in the World*, I told the Simon Potter story completely and, of course, shared "The God Memorandum" with my readers. I am so proud that the book has been in print, now, for more than twenty years and is used by hundreds of alcohol and drug rehabilitation programs around the world as its total sales approach five million copies in fifteen languages! Simon, it seems, is still rescuing humans from lives of grief and failure through his words and I am proud to have been his messenger, in a small way.

II

*L*ife was just not the same without Simon. In the days and weeks that followed his disappearance I ceased smiling at the world and the warm conversations of the past, especially with my staff, became little more than terse sentences. The sudden change in my behavior, of course, was obvious to everyone. Even the proud position as president of *Success Unlimited*, for which I had worked so hard, no longer excited me. I began spending much more time in my office with the door closed, often taking long naps in the afternoon on a leather couch while others, whom I had trained well, did most of the work in assembling each monthly issue. And every morning, after I pulled into our parking lot, I would catch myself looking for Simon among the parked cars while the sight of his old apartment building, fronting the lot, stirred all sorts of memories and sadness within me.

My life away from the magazine had also taken on unexpected twists. Since I was receiving more and more requests to deliver my speech on success and happiness to conventions and business gatherings, because *The Greatest Salesman in the World* was selling so well, I finally signed an exclusive contract with a very talented lady, Cheryl Miller. Her agency, Speakers International, was in a Chicago suburb and she began to book me so frequently, at ever increasing fees, that it didn't seem fair to the magazine for me to be away from the office as much as I was. Also, I signed my first three-book contract with Bantam Books for a new book manuscript to be delivered every fifteen months at a very substantial cash advance. It was strange that during that terrible period when I was feeling so down and blue, because Simon had vanished from my life, my two careers outside the magazine were flourishing more than ever.

Finally, after several long discussions with Bette, I decided to resign my presidency of *Success Unlimited*. W. Clement Stone, who owned the magazine, needed someone who was able to give all his or her effort and attention to putting out the very best possible publication each month and I was no longer doing that. I loved the man very much and he deserved better. I finally sent Mr. Stone a letter of resignation in the summer of '76, removed all the autographed photos of celebrities and award certificates from my office walls, packed them gently in boxes and departed two weeks after sending the letter, following a warm and tear-filled farewell party with all my staff. To this day I still have the tiny black and white television set that was presented to me as a parting gift. It was difficult to see through the tears, that evening, when I drove out of the old parking lot for the very last time. Simon Potter, where did you go?

To celebrate my freedom from corporate life we packed our two sons and some clothes in our car and drove to Scottsdale, Arizona, for a much-needed vacation. The area was as lovely as we remembered it from a previous trip and before the first week was over Bette and I were looking at new homes. We found a very special one, on an acre corner lot, still only half framed, and a very helpful Realtor, Marby Pruitt, who remains our good friend after all these years, reviewed the plans with us. After meeting with the builder, who agreed on the changes we wanted, we bought the place, went back to Illinois, put our house on the market, and sold it within a week! In early October we moved to Scottsdale and I gradually began to learn a new routine. No longer did I need to dress in a business suit, have breakfast, and drive more than twenty miles in heavy traffic in order to get to my office. Now I could climb into an old T-shirt and a pair of shorts, have breakfast in the kitchen overlooking our swimming pool, then step into the adjoining room, my writing studio, and I was at work! It took several months before I cured myself of always mentally planning my day at *Success Unlimited* while I showered and shaved. A new life was now upon us and I finally adjusted. I even commenced playing golf several times a week and Bette eventually acquired two large fabric stores in Phoenix and Scottsdale. A new life indeed!

The twelve or so years that followed our move to Arizona were both productive and gratifying. I wrote eight books, all of which have sold so well that they are still in print today and many of them, especially *The Choice, Mission: Success!*, and *A Better Way to Live* produce far more fan mail, each week, than I deserve.

My speech bookings continued to increase and

soon the speaking fee had advanced to the five digit area, which I found very difficult to realize. I can still remember having breakfast one morning with my oldest son, Dana, who was visiting us from his home in Flagstaff. Of course he knew that, along with the writing, his dad also flew around the country now and then giving speeches but he had no idea what I received in the way of compensation for those engagements. We were both eating breakfast cereal when he asked me, very casually, what they paid me for a speech. His mouth was full of cereal when I replied, "Twelve thousand dollars." He stared at me in wide-eyed disbelief, the cereal making strange gurgling sounds in his throat. "However," I continued, "you must remember that's for a whole hour." Then my very bright son reduced what I had said to terms he could handle. He said softly, "My God, Dad, that's two hundred dollars a minute! Sneeze or blow your nose and you make a hundred bucks!" I believe that Dana respected his old man a little more after that morning.

Simon would have been proud of me. In 1983 I received the C.P.A.E. award from the National Speakers Association, the highest speaking-honor bestowed by that fine organization, and one memorable evening in Chicago I was also presented with the 1983 Napoleon Hill Gold Medal for Literary Achievement. During the following year I became only the fourteenth member of the International Speakers Hall of Fame, joining such capable and talented individuals as Norman Vincent Peale, Rich DeVos, Art Linkletter, and Bob Richards. No big head. Bette would never have allowed it.

During those Arizona years I also toured the nation whenever a book of mine was published, promoting the new release on radio, television, and in the press. I estimate that I was interviewed approximately twelve hundred or more times and most of them were a lot of fun, including my six minutes of "celebrity" on the *Today* show.

Three of my books from that period were often discussed as possible movies: *The Gift of Acabar*, *The Christ Commission*, and *The Choice*. Michael Landon, before his untimely death, was seriously interested in doing *The Christ Commission* and the other two are still being considered by various interested parties.

Despite all my activity I often thought of Simon, especially after a great accomplishment like holding the first copy of a new book in my hands or receiving a long standing ovation after delivering my speech. Actually, the pain over his departure from my life had subsided with the years until, one day, UPS delivered a large, thin package to our house. Before I had completely opened the package an envelope fell out. I tore it open. It was from a prisoner who was writing to tell me how much *The Greatest Miracle in the World* had altered his outlook on life and his hope for the future. He was an artist, he wrote, and to show his thanks he was sending an oil painting of how he imagined Simon would look.

I held my breath as I carefully removed the thin layer of cloth that had been wrapped around the canvas panel until I found myself staring down at an almost perfect likeness of Simon holding a wine glass! I don't know how long I stared at the painting, with tears in my eyes, before I stood and placed it lovingly atop one of my bookcases, near my desk.

Later that day, after I had regained some control of my emotions, I wrote to the prisoner to thank him for his wonderful work and to ask him how he had decided on the likeness of Simon to use in the painting, since I hadn't described the old man that closely in the book. The answer I eventually received was short and simple. Before he had even commenced with the painting, he had fallen asleep one night, after rereading "The God Memorandum" from the book. As he slept he had a brief dream, a dream in which Simon appeared, saying, "You will be alright, you will be alright, you will be alright." The face that he painted was the image he had seen in his dream!

III

❧

I am convinced, and I've said so in countless interviews, that God is always playing chess with each of us. He makes moves in our life and then sits back to see how we react to the challenges.

In the summer of '88, God made a big move in our life although we didn't realize it at the time. Since I was booked for a speech at the Hynes Auditorium in Boston, Bette and I decided that we would take her mother and father with us and after we arrived in Boston we'd drive them to the tiny southern New Hampshire town where they had spent most of their lives before they had moved to Scottsdale to be close to their only daughter. We would leave them with Bette's uncle and also give them airline tickets which they could use in a couple of weeks to return to Arizona. Since neither of them enjoyed very good health we thought they would really appreciate returning to their old stamping grounds for one more journey down memory lane.

The trip east was uneventful. We rented a Town Car at Boston's Logan Airport and headed north, spending that night at the Ramada Inn in Concord, before delivering Nana and Gramps, on the following morning, to Bette's Uncle Bill in the small town of their youth which I will name, fictitiously, Langville, for this book.

Since we still had a day before we were expected in Boston, Bette and I went on a sentimental sight-seeing tour of her old hometown and the surrounding countryside, reminiscing and taking photos of the places we remembered from almost four decades ago when I was courting my pretty lady. What great memories! The only sadness was that all the giant elm trees that had made the tiny town's downtown area a green wonderland were gone, victims of Dutch elm disease.

As we were driving slowly through the sparsely populated pine and birch areas on the outskirts of town, we passed a narrow dirt road on our left. Bette slowed down and pointed at the rather large For Sale sign facing us at the mouth of the road. "You know, hon," she said, "in all the years I lived here as a kid I don't think I was ever down that road. I wonder what could possibly be for sale down there?"

She backed the Town Car until she had room and then turned slowly down the old road, which was so narrow that maple trees, from each side, reached across and mingled in an arch above our heads. After about a quarter mile we climbed a small rise and on our right was a solitary old white farmhouse with a For Sale sign out front. We pulled into the driveway and since there was no one around we brazenly went up to the windows and peeked inside. Fascinating! Old rough-hewn beams on the ceiling and large polished planks on the floor. It was very obvious that this lonely place had enjoyed plenty of tender loving care.

We were still looking inside when another car pulled into the driveway and a smiling man came bounding across the lawn. He introduced himself, said he lived up the road and was the Realtor handling this great house which had only gone on the market yesterday. He shook his head saying that because of the house's isolated location he thought it might have been weeks or even months before he had the chance to show the place to any prospects. Would we like to go inside and look around? Not really, we replied, we were just doing a little sight-seeing and already owned a lovely home in Scottsdale. Also, I said, if he had come by five minutes later we'd have been gone and he replied that perhaps it was all meant to be . . . that he was destined to catch us before we departed. I glanced at Bette who sighed and asked him to unlock the front door. We loved the house, every room. It needed a lot of work but so what? We could remodel it to our taste. Five hours later we answered God's move. We placed a deposit on the house!

At first our thoughts were that this wonderful old farm, hiding in the woods, would make a great summer place but one day, after we had returned home, we were driving to Phoenix to do some shopping when we saw a huge black cloud of pollution hanging over the city. That was all the nudge we needed. We decided to sell our Arizona home and move back east. The Realtor who had sold us the old farmhouse also had a very talented group of carpenters, plumbers, and electricians who worked for him and so we returned to New Hampshire, had several meetings with him, and finally gave the go-ahead on the remodeling plans plus the addition of a new three-car garage and a four-room apartment over it which would be for Nana and Gramps since we couldn't possibly leave the old folks behind in Arizona.

We got lucky, sold the Scottsdale home in exactly six months, and moved across the country in the fall of '89. As Bette said, while heavy cartons were being carried from the huge moving van into the old farmhouse, "Well, I'm not making very much progress in my life. Here I am, right back where I started, many years ago."

Before the first snowfall of the year we had pretty much settled into our new home. The carpenters and builders had done a masterful job in building the additional rooms and garage as well as remodeling many of the old sections of the house. I was especially proud of my new studio. What had once been an unfinished storage room next to the old kitchen, with daylight and moisture seeping through the rough wallboards, had been transformed, with our son Dana's clever plans and some skilled carpentry, into an insulated and carpeted, sunny, seven-window room, complete with fireplace and huge maple bookcases that extended at right angles from the east wall to hold all my books. In my book, *A Better Way to Live,* I had taken great pains to describe my studio in Scottsdale to the readers, but by the time the book was published, in 1990, we were no longer living in Scottsdale. I tried very hard to follow the book's description of that other studio by hanging photos and plaques on the new studio walls in pretty much the same arrangement as they had all hung in Scottsdale.

Our tiny dirt road, Blueberry Lane, joined with a tarred two-laner called Old Pound Road about a quarter of a mile east of our house and this was the place, among the pines, where God made another unexpected move in my life. At the very corner of Blueberry Lane and Old Pound Road, scores of large boulders had been piled atop each other, high and neatly, until they formed a corral of granite with an entrance at the rear. On one of the larger stones, facing Old Pound Road, was a bronze plaque indicating that this town pound had been erected in 1817 and restored in 1948. Apparently the northern portion of tiny Langville had been much more populous at the beginning of the nineteenth century and if anyone's animals wandered off the farm, the neighbor who retrieved them would walk them down to the Old Pound, lead them into the stone corral, and then block the rear opening with dead tree limbs so that the cows or horses or oxen or whatever would remain in the pound until their owner came to claim them.

Soon after we had settled in I renewed an old routine from Scottsdale and, almost every day, walked a mile or two after breakfast. One morning, as I was approaching the Old Pound, a red fox slowly and boldly crossed the road no more than twenty feet in front of me. I stopped and watched the little guy until he vanished beneath the bushes and then, instead of continuing on, I stepped off the road and went down the embankment until I was near the opening at the pound's rear. My first visit. I walked inside, hesitantly, the layers of leaves beneath my feet muffling all footstep sounds. I stood absolutely still, feeling the strange vibrations of centuries. My God, James Monroe, our fifth president, was inaugurated the year this pound was erected!

I don't remember how long I stood silently in the center of the pound before I heard a hoarse, basso profundo voice, very near to me. "Mister Og, you are looking wonderful!"

For a moment I felt sheer terror. Then I forced myself to turn slowly until I was facing an old man, leaning against the south wall, no more than ten yards away. He nodded and smiled and then he waved at me, urging me to come closer. I

held my breath and moved toward him, very
slowly at first, and then I ran the last few steps
until we were embracing each other. "Simon," I
cried. "Is it really you? Oh, how I have missed
you!"

The old man gently patted the back of my head
and nodded. "I know, I know. I have missed you,
too, Mister Og . . . with all my heart!"

IV

After several long sighs and embraces, Simon Potter led me to a lower section of the Old Pound wall and we sat close together, our right hands grasping each other's tightly. Except for a little less hair on top, the old man looked exactly the same as when I had last seen him in Chicago, and since we had celebrated his seventy-ninth birthday back then, before he disappeared, he was now around ninety-five years old. Amazing!

As we talked, I learned that Simon, through some mysterious means, had been following my activities closely for the past fifteen years or so despite our separation. I tested him on some of the more unusual events that had occurred in my life during the past several years and he never missed a fact. He even smiled and commented on the tactic I had used when I toured the country to promote *The Greatest Miracle in the World*. Whenever an interviewer would ask specific questions about the old ragpicker's authenticity in the book I would refer that person to the Bible and John 4:48 . . . "Then said Jesus unto him, except ye see signs and wonders, ye will not believe."

Somewhere during our dialogue I finally mustered enough courage to ask Simon why he had walked out of my life so suddenly, and he replied that an emergency had arisen and it seemed that he was the most qualified ragpicker to rescue a particular individual. He also explained that if he had told me he was departing, it would have been an even more painful event for both of us.

There was so much more I wanted to ask my old friend but just about then I heard a car coming up Old Pound Road and I could see that it was Bette in our Jeep Grand Wagoneer. I patted Simon's hand, stood, and ran up the embankment. As Bette turned the corner she saw me and hit the brake, scowling. I reached over, opened the car door and said, "Come on down in the pound, hon. There's someone special I want you to meet."

She followed me, not saying a word until we were finally standing close to the center of the stone enclosure. Simon had vanished.

Following the events of that unforgettable morning, the Old Pound became a special haven for me. During my walks each day I would stop at the corner of our road, step down the embankment into the pound and sit on one of the boulders for ten minutes or so, relishing the almost scary silence as well as the unseen birds singing high in the trees above. Of course I kept hoping and praying that Simon would reappear and one bright morning he did, greeting me as if he had never been gone. When I pressed him as to why he hadn't remained in the pound so that I could introduce him to Bette he shrugged his broad shoulders and replied that he didn't believe it would be wise to involve her in our relationship. As conditions stood she could truthfully say that she had never met or talked with Simon Potter. I started to ask him what difference it would make . . . but something prevented me.

Simon and I worked out a very special arrangement that morning. We decided that we would meet, at the Old Pound, every Tuesday morning when I was not away somewhere giving a speech. Hopefully we would be able to have long and enjoyable chats about life and what was happening in our world just as we once did in the old man's apartment. On one of our first Tuesdays together I remember boldly asking him if he was back in my life because I was about to need his special assistance. He smiled and shook his head and replied, "Mister Og, I am not following you for any reason. You must realize that I was already living here for about a year before you arrived."

Simon explained that when he decided he needed a drastic change in his life he had gone in search of a far more peaceful setting than Chicago. Since he remembered how I had often, in our talks, recalled the peace and beauty of New Hampshire, he had come to this special place and luckily discovered a small, one-room, old cottage in the nearby woods that he leased from a wealthy lady who resided in Francestown. That Bette and I had moved almost three thousand miles and bought an ancient farmhouse within a quarter of a mile of Simon's residence, he sighed, probably involved odds of many, many billion to one. It was, he said softly, indeed a wondrous miracle but he wanted me to understand that he was not following me nor was I in any danger that he could foresee.

One Tuesday morning, as we were chatting,

Simon removed the unlit old corncob pipe that
always dangled from the side of his mouth and
said, in a hesitating voice quite unlike him, that
he had a special favor to ask of me; however, he
would like to invite me to come to his nearby
home on the following Tuesday and while I was
there he would explain. He said he needed help
on a special project he had been trying to complete for many months and now he felt comfort-
able in asking me since he was convinced that
something stronger than fate had reunited us.

Simon's cottage was buried among the trees,
just off a small path but far enough into the
woods so that it was not visible from Old Pound
Road. Most of the interior furnishings of the neat
single room, Simon explained, were owned by the
nice lady who had leased the place to him but the
books, on several pine shelves, the "hand of God"
books, all belonged to him.

Simon must have been planning to invite me
for some time. From a small ice chest he removed
a bottle of white sherry and it was the old days all
over again, filled with laughter and good talk.
Finally, the old boy got around to explaining the
help he needed. He had been accumulating several boxes of notes dealing with what he believed
were the best methods of changing life's failures

into successful and happy individuals and he had been wondering if I would take his material and assemble his collection of wisdom into a very brief but powerful declaration of resolve that would benefit everyone who read it. He was currently in the process of selecting his best material and said he could have it all in my hands within a month. Then, if I was pleased with the finished product perhaps I might consider using it in a book as I had used "The God Memorandum" in *The Greatest Miracle in the World*. I agreed, without hesitation.

That day, just as I was departing from Simon's cottage, there was a tremendous crash on the roof. Simon just smiled and shook his head, saying, "My special friend has returned again. Come outside, Mister Og. You must see this."

Standing on the flimsy roof was the largest bird I have ever seen. Simon explained that it was a great blue heron who had managed to get himself snarled in the underbrush one day when Simon fortunately happened to come along and free him. The bird, since that morning, was forever bringing the old man cans and bottles and even flowers, usually dropping his "gifts" of gratitude on the roof. As Simon was explaining all this to me, the huge bird opened his beak and released an empty beer can which rolled noisily down off the roof and landed at our feet. Then he raised his huge wings and slowly flew off above the trees. Simon said that he had named the bird Franklin, after New Hampshire's only president, Franklin Pierce.

Several weeks later, as I was working at my desk, trying to catch up with my mail, there was a large thud on the studio roof. Thinking that the huge ash tree near our home had dropped another large branch, I raced outside. Franklin, the great blue heron, was standing very still at the edge of my roof, his head cocked to one side, studying me intently.

"Good morning, Mister Og!"

I should have known. Simon, carrying a large briefcase, was finally paying me a visit and, of course, Bette was in Concord for the morning, having her hair done. I gave the old boy a complete tour of our home after he had signed our guest book in the front hall, *Simon Potter*, and for his address, *The Planet Earth*. Finally, my studio. He had taken only a few steps inside the room when he paused and looked around. With very wide open eyes he turned to me and exclaimed that it looked exactly as I had described my Scottsdale studio in *A Better Way to Live*. I explained why. Finally, after Simon had moved slowly around the entire room, studying every wall plaque and trophy and framed autographed photographs from Charles Lindbergh to Michael Jackson, he opened his old briefcase and removed several sheets of paper, which he placed on the coffee table. After he had reviewed all his notes for several weeks, these, he said, were what he would like me to use in the special piece. My assignment . . . to write a powerful declaration of self-affirmation that one could read in six minutes or less, every morning, to launch that particular human on the proper course for a successful day. I told him I would try my best but to do it all in such a brief piece was asking a great deal. He nodded and patted me on the shoulder as if I were a child. "I'm certain you will succeed, Mister Og," he said smiling. Then he departed.

I completed the project in only a couple of weeks, titling the finished piece "For the Rest of My Life . . ." Simon's powerful thoughts had needed little rewriting or editing. On the Tuesday after Labor Day, as we had agreed, I delivered the finished work to him at the Old Pound. He slowly opened the brown envelope and removed my typed pages. At least fifteen minutes passed before he looked up at me, his old eyes filling with tears.

"It is everything I had hoped it would be,

Mister Og. I pray you will find it in your heart to use this in a future book."

His right hand caressed the wooden cross he always wore, hanging by a leather strap around his neck. He lifted the cross and strap over his head and handed them to me. I backed away but he was firm. He wanted me to have a part of him so that I would never forget him, as if that were possible. He then removed his old corncob pipe from his jacket pocket and said, "You take the cross. I still have my old pipe for solace." When I left him, because I was expecting an important call from my publisher, Simon was still sitting on the granite boulders rereading our words. All the specific details of our reunion in New Hampshire, after so many years apart, including Simon's very special motivational piece titled "For the Rest of My Life . . ." eventually appeared in the next book I wrote, *The Return of the Ragpicker*.

When I arrived home the very first thing I did was walk into my studio and hang Simon's cross on the special bulletin board behind my desk. Then, over a light lunch, I was telling Bette about my special morning with Simon when we heard a frightening crash on our roof. We both dashed out the kitchen door and there he was, Franklin, the great blue heron, staring down at us. Then he shook his head and something fell from his beak, rolling down the steeply pitched roof and tumbling into the grass. I reached down and picked up an old corncob pipe. I handed it to Bette, crying "No! No! No!" and began running down Blueberry Lane toward the Old Pound.

When Bette arrived at the pound she found me inside, sitting on the damp leaves, holding Simon's lifeless body in my arms and sobbing.

V

❦

*S*imon Potter was buried in our town's small cemetery, beneath a towering maple tree. The area's only undertaker, a kind and gentle old man, made it extremely easy for us by handling all the details including our purchase of the cemetery plot. Only Bette and I were at the open grave as the old ragpicker's casket, also containing his corn-cob pipe, was lowered slowly into the ground. We both cried. Less than a month later, Simon had his own small granite headstone. On its polished gray face, as per our instructions, the chiseled inscription read . . .

SIMON POTTER
1898–1993
Mizpah. May the Lord watch between me and thee,
when we are absent, one from another.

Fortunately, for my depressed and mourning state of mind, I got very busy soon after Simon's burial. My speech bookings crisscrossed the nation from Portland, Oregon, for Business Expo, to West Palm Beach for Fruit of the Loom, to Las Vegas for two appearances followed by a benefit for the Arizona State Gymnastics program with Willie Nelson also on the program, NU SKIN in Salt Lake City, and re Max in northern Indiana.

When my new book, *The Twelfth Angel*, was published, I took a break from my speeches and toured the country promoting the book on radio, on television, and in the press in more than a dozen cities. I was extremely busy and loving it, as I approached my seventieth birthday, until a routine physical examination at my doctor's set off all kinds of alarms when it was discovered, after several follow-up examinations and tests, that I had cancer of the prostate.

Since the cancer had not spread beyond the prostate, I opted to have the thing removed rather than have it treated by chemotherapy. However, while I was on the operating table the unexpected happened. I suffered several heart attacks! I was immediately rushed to the Dartmouth–Hitchcock Medical Center in Lebanon, New Hampshire, and, despite all the tubes protruding from my body plus a severe loss of blood during the prostate operation, it was decided that I could not survive more than thirty-six hours without immediate open-heart surgery and we could not wait until the body had regained some of its strength following the recent operation.

During my open-heart surgery, which lasted many hours, they replaced one vein plus the right aortic valve with a man-made one. I spent six weeks in the hospital, lost more than thirty pounds, and was home in time to spend Christmas with all my gang.

In the spring of 1994, after I had regained my strength without putting any unnecessary weight back on, I resumed my old schedule of speeches plus spending long hours at the typewriter, working on a new book when I was at home. I truly felt like my old self.

Then, in the spring of 1995, I found myself back in the hospital with something called endo-carditis, which, I learned later, is usually fatal. Apparently I had picked up a strange bacteria somewhere and it was multiplying in my veins and accumulating on my new heart valve. Eventually the valve would stop opening and closing with every heartbeat and I would die. The hospital's objective was to cleanse all the bacteria off the valve and to do this they pumped penicillin into my body every three hours, around the clock. I remember one period when I went twelve days without any solid food. I was much closer to death than I realized.

One evening, after I had dozed off, I had a strange experience. In a dream I saw Simon Potter. His corncob pipe protruded from the corner of his mouth and he was smiling and nodding at me, saying, over and over, "You will be alright, Mister Og! You will be alright, Mister Og!" During my hospital stay of almost seven weeks, I dreamt of Simon saying those same words on at least four or five occasions. I didn't know what to think and when I told Bette she just smiled and shook her head and said, "I think your guardian angel is still nearby, hon."

During the second hospital stay I lost another thirty pounds, so that big guy who weighed nearly 210 pounds before his original open-heart surgery now had a closet full of Italian silk suits for his speaking dates that all hung on his body like circus tents. What saddened me most were the countless speeches we had to cancel during my recovery period, especially an eight-speech junket to Australia, Hong Kong, Singapore, and Malaysia where the sponsors had even been willing to pay Bette's expenses to accompany me.

Within a few weeks after my hospital release I commenced an exercise program which was followed, almost every morning, by the same walk I had taken in past years, up our dirt road to the corner, then down Old Pound Road for perhaps a mile or so and return.

One morning, after my exercise, when I emerged from the house and started walking, I was confronted by a great blue heron standing rigidly in the road ahead and staring at me as if he had been waiting for me to make an appearance. As I drew closer, the huge bird turned and strutted ahead of me, pausing every now and then to glance back as if he were making certain that I was still following him.

When we arrived at the Old Pound, the bird made a right turn and continued his walk down Old Pound Road. 'My God,' I thought, 'he's leading me to Simon's old place. This must be Franklin!'

Once again the great blue heron paused and

looked back at me. Then he turned right and vanished from my sight. I knew he was now walking on the narrow path, overrun with ferns and tall grasses, that led to what had been Simon's home. When I arrived at the path, I also turned right, pushing my way gently through the giant masses of fireweed and wild blueberry bushes.

I finally broke into a clearing covered with tall grass and daisies. Twenty yards or so ahead of me Franklin had paused to glance back once more. Ahead of us, nearly surrounded by trees and bushes, was the shabby one-room cottage that had been Simon's final home. I swear that Franklin nodded at me and then he slowly raised his huge wings and flew off gracefully toward the west.

I approached the tiny old place very slowly and I know that my repaired heart was beating a lot faster than usual. Since Simon's death I had driven up and down Old Pound Road hundreds of times but I could never bring myself to stop and revisit the cabin site. It had been difficult enough just facing up to his death without inflicting any additional pain on myself.

The small cottage, little more than a shack, was now in shambles. All four windows had been smashed in and when I pushed on the only door, already partly open, I was confronted by a totally trashed interior. The narrow bed had been over-turned, its thin mattress lying on a floor covered with pieces of glass. The familiar burgundy-colored drapes, ripped from the windows, were in a pile near the door. Books were scattered everywhere and some had even been stuffed inside the small open refrigerator. The legs of Simon's small lunch table had been broken, there was a large boulder resting in the gray enamel sink and a pine log was protruding from the top of the small wood stove. Teenagers having fun? The place could not have been any more of a disaster if someone had ex-ploded a small bomb inside. How sad!

I walked slowly around the small room, trying to recall all the good moments we had in here, just visiting and talking. How fortunate we hu-mans are to have memories that are always so much more durable than the material things in our life. I picked up two soggy books and shook off slivers of glass. Thoreau's *Walden* and Franklin's *Autobiography*. Both great favorites of Simon, I re-membered. I leaned against a wall and closed my eyes. Should I have visited this place often? Would that have prevented this needless destruction? I don't know.

Close to where I had been standing, on the west side of the house, was the ragpicker's old rolltop desk that he had told me was the only piece of furniture he had moved from his Chicago apartment. It was still standing upright among all the debris and its rolltop cover was closed. Not knowing what I would find, I inhaled deeply, reached down and slowly pushed open the rolltop. There was nothing inside . . . no papers . . . no pens or pencils . . . not even a calendar . . . nothing except an old, tattered, fat loose-leaf notebook. A torn piece of yellow legal pad paper was held against the faded blue cover by a rusty paper clip. On the paper, handwritten in large letters, were two words . . . *Mister Og!*

VI

Clutching the old notebook tightly to my chest, I treaded carefully among the glass and debris until I was at the door. Outside I inhaled deeply several times and walked slowly home.

Bette was where I had left her when I had stepped out the kitchen door to commence my morning walk, upstairs in her sewing room working on a quilt. I made a cup of instant coffee and brought it into my studio along with the old notebook.

I sat at my desk for the longest time, slowly caressing the tattered cover of the notebook with my hands. Finally I opened it. On the first page of narrow-lined three-hole paper, written in graceful strokes of black ink, was a letter to me, undated. Once again, I thought, Simon's presence is in my studio. I took a long drag on my coffee cup before I began reading . . .

Dear Mister Og,

I fully realize that the odds are exceedingly high you will never read these words or the contents of this notebook and yet, although I have so very little of anything, I still have hope.

Since we first met in that snowy parking lot, so many years ago, your friendship has been a precious gift from God to me. In your very special book, *The Greatest Miracle in the World*, you were kind enough to include "The God Memorandum" that I had sent to you as well as write about our times together in Chicago. I am positive that your words have helped lift many souls out of their swamps of misery and despair. I am also hopeful that someday you will utilize that brief but powerful piece, "For the Rest of My Life . . ." that you wrote from my notes, perhaps when you decide to write the story of our unbelievable reunion here in New Hampshire after all these years.

Since your miraculous return to this most lovely part of the world, I have been tempted on many occasions to seek your opinion on the contents of this notebook which I have been working on, now and then, for many years. I dare not even attempt to estimate the number of hours I have toiled on the material contained in these pages yet I have never been able to bring myself to ask you to take the necessary time to read and evaluate the work and give me your honest opinion. Some day, perhaps, God will allow me the courage to show it to you but until then it will rest here, inside my old desk.

Mister Og, you are well aware of the books I have collected through the years, which I proudly call my "hand of God" books. From years of observation I had become convinced that the wisest and most powerful principles for success and a good life are not to be found, today, in even the largest of bookstores among all the countless rows of modern books with glaring covers which are classified as "motivational" or "self-help." Almost all of the authentic classics on how to live a good life, in peace, wealth, and security, are out of print and have been so for many years, sadly. Yet the basic and powerful truths about achieving success that they contained will endure forever.

After reading and reflection, for several years, I have carefully selected portions from several of the old "hand of God" masterpieces and assembled them into what I have dared to call *Advice from Heaven*. In a way, each of my choices might be considered a rung on the ladder of life since each contains specific observations and advice that I continue to believe was guided by God's hand. Hopefully, the reader will ascend from rung to rung until he or she has finally left all the harmful negatives behind and is standing proudly at the top of the ladder enjoying a new life of fulfillment and joy.

In preparing this work I was confronted with several challenges. The most difficult was taking the language of another age and rewriting it so that today's reader would not be hindered by archaic words and phrases from the past and yet preserving the author's original meaning. Another challenge was to remove the masculine tinge from all the writings, common in the literature of earlier generations, so that the messages would apply to today's women as well as their male counterparts. The third challenge was working out some logical system that I could use, now and then, to interrupt the original author and creator with comments of my own on a specific subject.

At long last, the rewriting has been completed to my satisfaction. I have also managed to remove most, if not all, of what we today would call the sexist tinge in some of the sentences and I have worked out a method of including my comments, whenever I feel they are necessary, by merely putting parenthesis marks around my words, in paragraphs of their own and initialed by me, to separate them from those of the original author.

If this manuscript is still in its resting place inside my old desk when I make my final departure from this world, then it will be up to heavenly forces to determine whether or not your eyes are ever to read my work so that you can decide whether or not it deserves to be shared with humanity. I can only pray.

Once again, Mizpah,

Simon

My hand was trembling as I turned the page and read . . .

Advice from Heaven

Dear reader . . . you are now holding in your hands what can be your guide to a better life. Use your imagination and think of this book and its message as if it were a unique ladder constructed in heaven, one which will take you high above the failure and futility you have endured in the past until you eventually reach a new plateau filled with joy and pride and success.

The advice and guidance contained on each rung of this special heavenly ladder is certain to assist and guide you to reach for the next rung and the next until you finally have the know-how and motivation to transform your life into all you have dreamed it could be.

These present moments, now, may be the most important of your life. Find a peaceful location, so that you will not be distracted, and read what is to follow on "The First Rung of Life's Ladder." Read slowly. Consider the wise counsel it contains and let those words guide and shape your actions in the days that follow.

Look at a calendar. Circle today's date. Next week, on the same day of the week, take the time to read both "The First Rung of Life's Ladder" and "The Second Rung of Life's Ladder." A week later, read "The Second Rung of Life's Ladder" and "The Third Rung of Life's Ladder" and continue with this special technique until you finally arrive at the top rung, the very pinnacle, much closer to peace and happiness and heaven. What you then do is entirely up to you. If you are satisfied with your progress since you took your first step on the ladder, then set this book aside in a place where it can be retrieved quickly if needed. Treat it as you would the spare tire on your automobile. If and when you find yourself slipping back into your old way of life or struggling to overcome some unexpected adversity, just open the book to the first rung and commence your upward climb in the same way again. Not difficult and you won't regret it.

At last ... at long last ... your life and your future are in your hands alone. You now possess the power, the knowledge, and the means to make all your tomorrows a special and unique heaven on earth.

You deserve a better way of life. At last your future is in your hands. Live it well!

VII

✤✤✤

THE FIRST RUNG OF
LIFE'S LADDER

*H*is name was Orison Swett Marden. The
words you are about to read as you ascend the
first and second rungs of life's ladder have been
taken from his classic book, *Pushing to the Front*,
whose first edition was published in 1883. Yes . . .
1883, and it remained a bestseller for more than a
decade, both in this country and abroad.

How fortunate we are that this wise man of
yesterday can still communicate with us. As you
read his words you will hopefully learn two very
important principles that are vital in your quest
for a brighter future. The first is that the opportunity for a better life is available right where you

are, right now! Success and the good life are not far off, at the end of some rainbow, they are much closer to you, right in your own neighborhood!

When you arrive on the second rung of life's ladder you will also be reminded by the same author that many of the most successful individuals in the world were not above the average in ability but were only ordinary people who refused to live a life of failure. For your own good, please heed his words. Brooding over the past or idly dreaming about tomorrow are both futile pursuits. In order to advance upward on this special ladder, now within your reach, you must seize the present moment, no matter what your age may be.

If you are deficient in education, if you were lacking in early advantages, if you have a low supply of nerve, grit, or courage, if you are timid, sensitive, or lack initiative, the words that follow will help you to overcome these defects. If you feel that your life has been a failure, that you have never found your place, that there is success for others but not for you, if you have lost your grip on life, your confidence in yourself or in your fellow man, pay special attention to Mr. Marden's declarations and let them lead you up the ladder of life. Take heart! Soon you will be on your way with a torch that will kindle the smoking flax of ambition into a living flame that will cast a halo around the rest of your days. S. P.)

"Good chances for the young no longer exist as formerly," complained a youthful law student to Daniel Webster. "You are mistaken," replied the great statesman and jurist, "there is always room at the top."

No chance? No opportunities? In a land where thousands of children eventually become very rich, where newsboys go to Congress, and where those born in the lowest stations attain the highest positions? The world is all gates, all opportunities, to those who will use them. But, like Bunyan's Pilgrim in the dungeon of Giant Despair's castle—who had the key of deliverance all the time with him but had forgotten it—we fail to rely wholly upon our ability to achieve all that is good for us, which has been given to the weakest as well as the strongest. We depend too much on outside assistance. We look too high, for things close by.

A Baltimore lady lost a valuable diamond bracelet at a ball, and supposed that it was stolen from the pocket of her cloak. Years afterward she washed the steps of the Peabody Institute, pondering how to get money to buy food. She cut up an old, worn-out, ragged cloak to make a hood, when lo! in the lining of the cloak she discovered the diamond bracelet. During all her poverty she was worth $3,500, but did not know it!

Many of us who think we are poor are actually rich in opportunities, if we can only see them, in possibilities all about us, in faculties worth more than diamonds. In our large Eastern cities it has been learned that at least ninety-four out of every hundred found their first fortune at home, or near at hand, and in meeting common, every-day wants. <u>It is a sorry day for those who cannot see any opportunities where they are but think they can do better somewhere else.</u>

(Note that I have underlined the previous sentence because of its importance. I shall use that method whenever I believe it is necessary to reinforce the author's statement. S. P.)

Some Brazilian shepherds organized a party to go to California to dig gold, and took along a handful of translucent pebbles to play checkers with on the voyage. After arriving in San Francisco, and after having thrown away most of the pebbles, they discovered that they were diamonds. They hastened back to Brazil, only to find that the mines from which the pebbles had been gathered had been taken up by other prospectors and sold to the government.

The richest gold and silver mine in Nevada was sold by the owner for $42, to get money to pay his passage to other mines where he thought he could get rich. Professor Agassiz once told his Harvard students of a farmer who owned a farm of hundreds of acres of unprofitable woods and rocks, and concluded to sell out and get into a more profitable business. He decided to go into the coal-oil business; he studied coal measures and coal-oil deposits, and experimented for a long time. He sold his farm for $200, and engaged in his new business two hundred miles away. Only a short time after, the man who bought his farm discovered upon it a great flood of coal-oil, which the farmer in ignorance of its value had previously tried to drain off.

Hundreds of years ago there lived near the shore of the river Indus a Persian by the name of Ali Hafed. He lived in a cottage on the river bank, from which he could get a grand view of the beautiful country stretching away to the sea. He had a wife and children, an extensive farm, fields of grain, gardens of flowers, orchards of fruit, and miles of forest. He had plenty of money and everything that the heart could wish. He was contented and happy. One evening a priest of Buddha visited him, and, sitting before the fire, explained to him how the world was made, and how the first beams of sunlight condensed on the earth's surface into diamonds.

The old priest told that a drop of sunlight the size of his thumb was worth more than large mines of copper, silver, or gold; that with one of them he could buy many farms like his; that with a handful he could buy a province, and with a mine of diamonds he could purchase a kingdom. Ali Hafed listened, and was no longer a rich man. He had been touched with discontent, and with that all wealth vanishes.

Early the next morning he woke the priest who had been the cause of his unhappiness, and anxiously asked him where he could find a mine of diamonds. "What do you want of diamonds?" asked the astonished priest. "I want to be rich and place my children on thrones." "All you have to do is go and search until you find them," said the priest. "But where shall I go?" asked the now poor farmer. "Go anywhere, north, south, east, or west." "How shall I know when I have found the place?" "When you find a river running over the white sands between high mountain ranges, in those white sands you will find diamonds," answered the priest.

The discontented man sold the farm for what he could get, left his family with a neighbor, took the money he had at interest, and went to search for the coveted treasure. Over the mountains of Arabia, through Palestine and Egypt, he wandered for years but found no diamonds. When his money was all gone and starvation stared him in the face, ashamed of his folly and of his rags, poor Ali Hafed threw himself into the tide and was drowned. The man who bought his farm was a contented man, who made the most of his surroundings and did not believe in going away from home to hunt for diamonds or success. While his camel was drinking in the garden one day, he noticed a flash of light from the white sands of the brook. He picked up a pebble, and pleased with its brilliant hues took it into the house, put it on the shelf near the fireplace, and forgot all about it.

The old priest of Buddha, who had filled Ali Hafed with the fatal discontent, called one day upon the new owner of the farm. He had no sooner entered the room than his eye caught that flash of light from the stone. "Here's a diamond!

Here's a diamond!" he shouted in great excite-
ment. "Has Ali Hafed returned?" "No," said the
farmer, "nor is that a diamond. That is but a
stone." They went into the garden and stirred up
the white sand with their fingers and behold,
other diamonds more beautiful than the first
gleamed out of it. So the famous diamond beds of
Golconda were discovered. Had Ali Hafed been
content to remain at home and dig in his own
garden, instead of going abroad in search for
wealth, he would have been one of the richest
men in the world, for the entire farm abounded in
the richest of jewels.

You have your own special place and work. Find
it, fill it. Scarcely anyone who reads these lines
but has a much better opportunity to win success
than Garfield, Wilson, Franklin, Lincoln, Harriet
Beecher Stowe, and thousands of others had. But
to succeed you must be prepared to seize and
improve the opportunity when it comes. <u>Remem-
ber that four things come not back: the spoken
word, the sped arrow, the past life, and the neglected opportunity.</u>

It is one of the paradoxes of civilization that the
more opportunities are utilized, the more new ones
are thereby created. New openings are as easy to
find as ever to those who do their best; although it

is not so easy as formerly to obtain great distinction in the old lines, because the standard has advanced so much and competition has so greatly increased. "The world is no longer clay," said Emerson, "but rather iron in the hands of its workers and so we now must hammer out a place for ourselves by steady and rugged blows."

Thousands have made fortunes out of trifles which others pass by. As the bee gets honey from the same flower from which the spider gets poison, so some of us will get a fortune out of the commonest and meanest things such as scraps of leather, cotton waste, slag, iron filings, from which others get only poverty and failure. There is scarcely a thing which contributes to the welfare and comfort of humanity, scarcely an article of household furniture, a kitchen utensil, an article of clothing or of food, that is not capable of an improvement in which there may be a fortune.

Opportunities? They are all around us. Forces of nature plead to be used in the service of mankind, as lightning for ages tried to attract our attention to the great force of electricity, which would do our drudgery and leave us to develop the God-given powers within us. There is power lying latent everywhere waiting for the observant eye to discover it.

First find out what the world needs and then supply the want. An invention to make smoke go the wrong way in a chimney might be a very ingenious thing, but it would be of no use to humanity. The patent office at Washington is full of wonderful devices of ingenious mechanism, but not one in hundreds is of use to the inventor or to the world. And yet how many families have been impoverished, and have struggled for years amid want and woe, while the father has been working on useless inventions.

An observing man, the eyelets of whose shoes pulled out, but who could not afford to get another pair, said to himself, "I will make a metallic lacing hook, which can be riveted into the leather." He was then so poor that he had to borrow a sickle to cut grass in front of his hired tenement. He became a very rich man.

An observing barber in Newark, New Jersey, thought he could make an improvement on shears for cutting hair, invented clippers and became very rich. A Maine man was called in from the hayfield to wash clothes for his invalid wife. He had never before realized what it is to wash. Finding the method slow and laborious, he invented the washing machine and made a fortune. A man who was suffering terribly with a toothache felt that surely there must be some way of filling teeth which would prevent their aching and he invented the method of gold filling for teeth.

The great things of the world have not been accomplished by people of large means. The cotton-gin was first manufactured in a log cabin. John Harrison, the great inventor of the marine chronometer, began his career in the loft of an old barn. Parts of the first steamboat ever run in America were set up by Fitch in the vestry of a church in Philadelphia. McCormick began to make his famous reaper in a gristmill. The first model dry-dock was made in an attic. Clark, the founder of Clark University in Worcester, Massachusetts, began his great fortune by making toy wagons in a horse shed. Edison began his experiments in a baggage car on the Grand Trunk Railroad when a newsboy.

Michelangelo found, among waste rubbish beside a street in Florence, a piece of discarded Carrara marble, which some unskilled workman had cut, hacked, spoiled, and thrown away. No doubt other artists had noticed the fine quality of the marble, and regretted that it should have been spoiled. But Michelangelo still saw an angel in the ruin and with his chisel and mallet he called out from it one of the finest pieces of statuary that man has ever created, the young David.

Patrick Henry was called a lazy boy, a good-for-nothing farmer, and he failed as a merchant. He studied law for six weeks and then put out his shingle. When he won his first case it dawned on him, finally, that he might possibly be a success even in his homeland in Virginia. After the Stamp Act was passed, Henry was elected to the Virginia House of Burgesses, and introduced his famous resolution against the unjust taxation of the American colonies. Eventually he became the most brilliant orator in America.

The great natural philosopher, Faraday, who was the son of a blacksmith, wrote, when a young man, to Humphry Davy, asking for employment at the Royal Institution. Davy consulted a friend on the matter. "Here is a letter from a young man named Faraday; he has been attending my lectures, and wants me to give him employment at the Royal Institution—what can I do?" "Do? Put him to washing bottles. If he is good for anything he will do it directly. If he refuses he is good for nothing." But the boy who would experiment in the attic of an apothecary shop with an old pan and glass vials during every moment he could snatch from his work saw in washing bottles an opportunity which in time led to a professorship at the Royal Academy at Woolwich. Tyndall said of this boy with no chance, "He is the greatest experimental philosopher the world has ever seen!" He became the wonder of his age in science.

There is a legend of an artist who long sought after a piece of sandalwood, out of which to carve a Madonna. He was about to give up in despair, leaving the vision of his life unrealized, when in a dream he was bidden to carve his Madonna from a block of oak wood which was destined for the fire. He obeyed and produced from a log of common firewood a masterpiece. Many of us lose great opportunities in life by waiting to find sandalwood for our carvings when they really lie hidden in the common logs that we burn. One person goes through life without seeing chances for doing anything great while another, standing nearby, snatches from the same circumstances and privileges opportunities for supreme achievement.

<u>It is a sorry day for those who cannot see opportunities where they are but think they can do better somewhere else.</u>

We cannot, all of us, make great discoveries like Newton, Faraday, and Edison or paint immortal pictures like Michelangelo or Raphael. But we can all make our lives sublime, <u>by seizing common occasions and making them great.</u>

If you want to get rich, study yourself and your own wants. You will find that millions of others have the same wants. The safest business is always connected with our prime necessities. We must have clothing and a dwelling. We must eat. We want comforts, facilities of all kinds for pleasure, education, and culture. Anyone who can supply a great want of humanity, improve any methods which men and women use, supply any demand of comfort, or contribute in any way to human well-being, can make a fortune. <u>And, that fortune can be made right where you are now!</u>

VIII

❧

THE SECOND RUNG OF
LIFE'S LADDER

*M*ost people do not face life in the right way. They neutralize a large part of their effort because their mental attitude does not correspond with their endeavor, so that while working for one thing they are really expecting something else. They do not approach their work with that assurance of victory which attracts, which forces results, that determination and confidence which knows no defeat.

To be ambitious for wealth and yet always expecting to be poor, to be forever doubting your ability to get what you long for, is like trying to

reach east by traveling west. There is no philosophy which can guide people to success when
they are always doubting their ability, and thus
attract failure instead.

<u>You will go in the direction in which you face.</u> If
you look toward poverty, toward lack, you will go
that way. If, on the other hand, you turn squarely
around and refuse to have anything to do with
poverty—to think it, live it, or recognize it—you
will then begin to make progress toward the goal
of plenty.

As long as you radiate doubt and discourage-
ment you will be a failure. If you want to get away
from poverty, you must keep your mind in a productive, creative condition. In order to do this you
must think confident, cheerful, creative thoughts.
The model must precede the statue. <u>You must see
a new world before you can live it.</u>

(Nearly a century after these wise words were
written, men with wisdom and experience such as
Napoleon Hill were telling a new generation that
their thoughts could make them rich. The line
between failure and success is usually so fine that
we scarcely know when we pass it; so fine that we
are often on the line and do not know it. How
many people have thrown up their hands at a
time when a little more effort, a little more

patience, would have achieved success? As the tide goes clear out, so it comes clear in. There is no failure except in no longer trying. Success is always achieved by those who try, and keep trying. As Longfellow once wrote, "the lowest ebb is when the tide turns." S. P.)

If those who are down in the world, who are sidetracked, who believe that their opportunity has gone forever, that they can never get on their feet again, only knew the power of reversal of thought they could easily get a new start.

"Is it possible to cross the path?" asked Napoleon of the engineers who had been sent to explore the dreaded pass of St. Bernard. "Perhaps," was the hesitating reply, "it is within the limits of *possibility*." "Forward then," said the little Corporal, without heeding their account of apparently insurmountable difficulties. England and Austria laughed in scorn at the idea of transporting across the Alps, where "no wheel had ever rolled, or by any possibility could roll," an army of sixty thousand men, with ponderous artillery, tons of cannon balls and baggage, and all the bulky munitions of war.

After this "impossible" deed had been accomplished, men saw that it might have been done long before. Previous commanders had excused themselves from encountering such gigantic obstacles by calling them insuperable. Many others had possessed the necessary supplies, tools, and rugged soldiers, but all lacked the grit and resolution of Bonaparte.

History furnishes thousands of examples of those who have seized occasions to accomplish results deemed impossible by those less resolute. True, there has been but one Napoleon, but, on the other hand, the mountains that challenge the average American are not as high or dangerous as the summits crossed by the great Corsican.

<u>Don't wait for extraordinary opportunities. Seize common occasions and make them great!</u>

"If you will let me try, I think I can make something that will do," said a boy who had been employed as a kitchen laborer at the mansion of Signor Faliero, as the story goes. A large number of society folk had been invited to a banquet and just before dinner was served the confectioner, who had been making a large ornament for the table, sent word that he had spoiled the piece. "You!" exclaimed the head servant in astonishment, "and who are you?" "I am Antonio Canova, the grandson of Pisano, the stone-cutter," replied the pale-faced little fellow.

"And pray, what can you do?" asked the major-domo. "I can make you something that will do for the middle of the table if you'll let me try." The servant was at his wits' end, so he told Antonio to go ahead and see what he could do. Calling for some butter, the young kitchen worker hastily molded a large, crouching lion, which the admiring major-domo placed upon the table.

Dinner was announced, and many of the most noted merchants, princes, and noblemen of Venice were ushered into the dining room. Among them were skilled critics of art work. When their eyes fell upon the butter lion, they forgot the purpose for which they had come, in their wonder at such a work of genius. They looked at the lion long and carefully and asked Signor Faliero what great sculptor had been persuaded to waste his skill upon such a temporary material. Faliero did not know so he called the head servant who brought Antonio before the company.

When the distinguished guests learned that the lion had been made in a short time by a young servant, the dinner was turned into a feast in his honor. The rich host declared that he would pay the lad's expenses under the best masters and he kept his word. Antonio was not spoiled by his good fortune but remained at heart the same simple, earnest, faithful boy who had tried so hard to become a good stone-cutter in the shop of Pisano. Some may not have heard how the boy Antonio took advantage of this first great opportunity but Canova eventually became one of the greatest sculptors of his time.

<u>Those who are weak, wait for opportunities, those who are strong, make them.</u>

Opportunities! Your life is full of them. Every lesson in school, every hour at the factory or the office, presents new opportunities. Every customer is an opportunity. Every newspaper article is an opportunity. Every client is an opportunity. Every sermon is an opportunity. Every business transaction is an opportunity—an opportunity to be polite—an opportunity to be kind—an opportunity to be honest—an opportunity to make another friend. Every proof of confidence in you is a great opportunity. Every responsibility thrust upon your strength and your honor is priceless. If a slave like Frederick Douglass, who at one time did not even own his body, could elevate himself into an orator, editor, and statesman, what can you achieve with all your rich opportunities compared with Douglass?

It is the idle person, not the great worker, who is always complaining that there is no time or opportunity. Yet, some will make more out of the odds and ends of opportunities which many carelessly toss away than others will get out of a whole lifetime. Like bees, they extract honey from every flower. Every person they meet, every circumstance of the day, adds something to their store of useful knowledge or personal power.

"There is nobody whom Fortune does not visit at least once in their life," said a wise author, "but when she finds that they are not ready to receive her, she goes in at the door and out at the window."

Young Philip Armour joined the long caravan of Forty-Niners and crossed the great desert with all his possessions in a prairie schooner drawn by mules. Hard work and steady gains in the mines enabled him to start, six years later, in the grain and warehouse business in Milwaukee. In nine years he made five hundred thousand dollars. But he saw his great opportunity in General Grant's order, "On to Richmond." One morning in 1864 he knocked at the door of his partner in his venture as a pork packer. "I am going to take the next train to New York," said he, "to sell pork 'short.' Grant and

Sherman have the southern rebellion by the throat and pork will go down to twelve dollars a barrel." This was his opportunity. He went to New York and offered pork in large quantities at forty dollars per barrel. It was eagerly taken. The shrewd Wall Street speculators laughed at the young Westerner and told him pork would go to sixty dollars, for the war was not nearly over. Mr. Armour, however, kept on selling and Grant kept on advancing. Richmond fell and pork fell with it to twelve dollars a barrel and Mr. Armour cleared two million dollars!

Opportunity! John D. Rockefeller saw his opportunity in petroleum. He could see that there was a large population in this country with very poor home lighting. Petroleum was plentiful but the refining process was so crude that the product was inferior and not wholly safe. Here was Rockefeller's chance. Taking into partnership Samuel Andrews, a porter in a machine shop where both men had worked, he started a single barrel "still" in 1870, using an improved process discovered by his partner. They made a superior grade of oil and prospered rapidly. In twenty years the business of the little refinery, scarcely worth one thousand dollars for building and apparatus, had grown into Standard Oil, capitalized at ninety million dollars. Mr. Rockefeller eventually became one of the richest men in the civilized world.

Are you prepared for your great opportunity?

Hawthorne dined one day with Longfellow and brought a friend with him from Salem. After dinner the friend said, "I have been trying to persuade Hawthorne to write a story based upon a legend of Acadia, and still current there—the legend of a girl who, in the dispersion of the Acadians, was separated from her lover. She passed her life in waiting and seeking for him and finally found him, dying in a hospital, when they were both very old." Longfellow wondered that the legend did not strike the fancy of Hawthorne and he said to him, "If you have really made up your mind not to use it for a story, will you let me have it for a poem?" To this Hawthorne consented and promised, moreover, not to treat the subject in prose till Longfellow had seen what he could do with it in verse. Longfellow seized his opportunity and gave the world "Evangeline."

Open eyes will discover opportunities everywhere, in your home, in your yard, in your neighborhood, in your town; open ears will never fail to detect the cries of those in need of assistance; open hearts will never want for worthy objects upon which to bestow their gifts and open hands will never lack for noble work to do.

Everybody had noticed the overflow when a solid is immersed in a vessel filled with water, although no one had made use of the knowledge that the body displaces its exact bulk of liquid; but when Archimedes observed the fact he perceived therein an easy method of finding the cubical contents of objects, however irregular in shape.

There was not a sailor in Europe who had not wondered what might lie beyond the Western Ocean, but it remained for Columbus to steer boldly out into an unknown sea and discover a new world.

Innumerable apples had fallen from trees, often hitting heedless men on the head as if to set them thinking, but Newton was the first to realize that they fall to the earth by the same law which holds the planets on their courses and prevents the momentum of all the atoms in the universe from hurling them wildly back to chaos.

Lightning had dazzled the eyes and thunder had jarred the ears of men since the days of Adam, in the vain attempt to call their attention to the all-pervading and tremendous energy of electricity; but the discharges of Heaven's artillery were seen and heard only by the eye and ear of terror until Franklin, by a simple experiment, proved that lightning is but one manifestation of a resistless yet controllable force, abundant as air and water.

"What is its name?" asked a visitor in a studio when shown, among many gods, one whose face was concealed by hair and which had wings on its feet. "Opportunity," replied the sculptor. "Why is its face hidden?" "Because men seldom know him when he comes to them." "Why has he wings on his feet?" "Because he is soon gone, and once gone, cannot be overtaken."

"Opportunity has hair in front," says a Latin author; "behind she is bald. If you seize her by the forelock, you may hold her, but, if suffered to escape, not Jupiter himself can catch her again."

Do not believe that ambition is a quality born within you; that it is not susceptible to improvement; that it is something thrust upon us which will take care of itself like the color of our eyes or the height of our body. Ambition requires constant care and education, just as the faculty for music or art does, or it will atrophy.

If we do not try to realize our ambition, it will

not keep sharp and defined. Our faculties become dull and soon lose their power if they are not exercised. How can we expect our ambition to remain fresh and vigorous through years of inactivity, indolence, or indifference? If we constantly allow opportunities to slip by us without making any attempt to grasp them, our inclination will grow duller and weaker.

"What I most need," said Emerson, "is somebody to make me do what I can." To do what I can, that is my problem; not what a Napoleon or a Lincoln could do, but what I can do! It makes all the difference in the world to us whether we bring out the best thing in us or the worst—whether we utilize ten, fifteen, twenty-five or ninety percent of our ability.

Everywhere we see people who have reached middle life or later without ever having been aroused enough to seize an opportunity. They have developed only a small percentage of their success possibilities. They are still in a dormant state. The best thing in them lies so deep that it has never been awakened. Never, never allow yourself to lapse into that sad condition!

The trouble with us is that we are always looking for a princely chance of acquiring riches, or fame, or worth. We expect mastery without apprenticeship, knowledge without study, and riches by credit. Born in an age and country in which knowledge and opportunity abound as never before, how can you sit with folded hands, asking God's help in work for which He has already given you the necessary faculties and strength?

With the world full of work that needs to be done; with human nature so constituted that often a pleasant word or a trifling assistance may stem the tide of disaster for some fellow man, or clear his path to success; with our own faculties so arranged that in honest, earnest, persistent endeavor we find our highest good; and with countless noble examples, to encourage us to dare and do, each moment brings us to the threshold of some new opportunity.

Don't wait for your opportunity. <u>Make it</u>—make it as Napoleon made his in a hundred "impossible" situations or as the shepherd-boy Ferguson made his when he calculated the distances of the stars with a handful of glass beads on a string. Make it, as all leaders have made their chances of success. Golden opportunities are nothing to laziness, but industry makes the commonest chances golden.

(When you make up your mind that you are done with your mediocre existence forever; that you will have nothing more to do with it; that you are going to erase every trace of it from your clothing, your personal appearance, your manner, your talk, your actions, your home; that you are going to show the world your real mettle; that you are no longer going to pass for a failure; that you have set your face persistently toward better things—a competence, an independence— and that nothing on earth can turn you from your resolution, you will be amazed to find what an uplifting power will come to you, what an increase of confidence, reassurance, and self-respect.

Resolve with all the vigor you can muster, while you are still only on this second rung of your magic ladder, that since there are plenty of good things in the world for everybody, you are going to have your share, without injuring anybody else or keeping others back. It was intended that you should have a competence, an abundance. It is your birthright. You are now becoming organized for success and conditioned for happiness and you should resolve to reach your own divine destiny!

Opportunities for success are in your own backyard!

Opportunities for success are in your own backyard!

Opportunities for success are in your own backyard! S. P.)

❦

IX

THE THIRD RUNG OF
LIFE'S LADDER

*D*uring his highly acclaimed career, nearly a century ago, Arnold Bennett wrote more than eighty books including his great classic *The Old Wives' Tale* as well as countless plays, journals, and articles. He lived such a full and happy life that he was often asked how he managed to accomplish so much and still find time to pursue so many other pleasures such as painting, music, and the theater. In response he wrote a small book, *How to Live on 24 Hours a Day,* published in 1907, containing his wise suggestions on how best to use the most valuable asset we all possess—time—to produce for us the greatest possible good.

This is one of the most important rungs on your ladder of life. You must learn how to invest your time wisely or you will never be able to achieve anywhere near your full potential. Remember the wise words of Horace Mann, "Lost: somewhere between sunrise and sunset, two golden hours, each set with sixty diamond minutes. No reward is offered, for they are gone forever." S. P.)

It has been said that time is money. That proverb understates the case. Time is a great deal more than money—usually. But though you might have the wealth of royalty you cannot buy yourself a minute more time than I have, or the cat by the fireplace has.

Philosophers have explained space. They have not explained time. Yet, it is the inexplicable raw material of everything. With it, all is possible; without it, nothing. The supply of time is truly a daily miracle, an affair genuinely astonishing when one examines it. You wake up in the morning, and lo! your purse is magically filled with twenty-four hours of the unmanufactured tissue of the universe of your life! It is yours. It is the most precious of possessions. Yet, no one can take it from you. It is unstealable. <u>And no one received either more or less than you receive!</u>

Talk about an ideal democracy! In the realm of time there is no aristocracy of wealth, and no aristocracy of intellect. Genius is never rewarded by even an extra hour a day. And there is no punishment. Waste your infinitely precious commodity as much as you will and the supply will still not be withheld from you. No mysterious power will say, "You are a fool. You do not deserve time and you shall be cut off at the meter." Also, you cannot draw on the future. It is impossible to get into debt! You cannot waste tomorrow; it is kept for you. You cannot waste the next hour; it is kept for you.

I said the affair was a miracle. Is it not?

You have to live on this twenty-four hours of daily time. Out of it you have to spin health, pleasure, money, content, respect, and the evolution of your immortal soul. Strange that the newspapers and magazines, so enterprising and up-to-date as they are, are not full of "How to live on a given income of time," instead of "How to live on a given income of money"! Money is far commoner than time.

If one can't contrive to live on a certain income of money, one earns a little more, or borrows it, or maybe even steals it. But if one cannot arrange that an income of twenty-four hours a day shall exactly cover all proper items of expenditure, one does make a mess of one's life.

Which of us lives on twenty-four hours a day? And when I say "lives" I do not mean exists, nor "muddles through." Which of us is free from that uneasy feeling that the "great spending departments" of his or her daily life are not managed as they ought to be? Which of us has not been saying, year after year, "I shall fix this or that when I have a little more time"?

We never shall have any more time. We have, and we have always had, all the time there is. It is the realization of this profound and neglected truth, which, by the way, is not my discovery, that has led me to examine how we spend our allotment of daily time.

(Failures always seem to act as if they had a thousand years to live. They drink too much, party too much, sleep too much, play too much, and constantly assure us that they will take care of all their duties tomorrow. There is no such thing as a calendar with a "tomorrow" on it. On her deathbed, the first Queen Elizabeth was heard to whisper, "All my possessions for just another moment of time." S. P.)

There is an innumerable band of souls who are

haunted, painfully, by the feeling that the years slip by, and slip by, and slip by, and that they have not been able to get their lives into proper working order. If we analyze that feeling we shall perceive it to be, primarily, one of uneasiness, of expectation, of looking forward, of aspiration. It is a source of constant discomfort. If we further analyze that feeling, even in ourselves, we shall see that it springs from a fixed idea that we ought to do something in addition to those things which we are loyally and morally obliged to do. We are obliged, by various codes written and unwritten, to maintain ourselves and our families, if any, in health and comfort, to pay our debts, to save, to increase our prosperity by increasing our efficiency. A task sufficiently difficult! A task which very few of us achieve! A task often beyond our skill! And even when we realize that the task is beyond our skill, that our powers cannot cope with it, we feel that we would be less discontented if we gave our powers, already overtaxed, something still further to do.

And such is, indeed, the fact. The wish to accomplish something outside their normal schedule is common to all human beings who, in the course of evolution, have risen past a certain level.

Until an effort is made to satisfy their wish, the

sense of uneasy waiting for something to start which has not started will remain to disturb the peace of the soul. That wish has been called by many names. It is one form of the universal desire for knowledge. And it is so strong that many whose lives have been given to the systematic acquirement of knowledge have been driven by it to overstep the limits of their program in search of still more knowledge.

Now that I have succeeded, if succeeded I have, in persuading you to admit to yourself that you are constantly haunted by a suppressed dissatisfaction with your own arrangement of your daily life; and that the primal cause of that inconvenient dissatisfaction is the feeling that you are every day leaving undone something which you would like to do, and which, indeed, you are always hoping to do when you have "more time"; and now that I have drawn your attention to the glaring, dazzling truth that you will never have "more time," since you already have all the time there is—you expect me to let you into some wonderful secret by which you may, at any rate, approach the ideal of a perfect arrangement of the day, and by which, therefore, that haunting, unpleasant daily disappointment of things left undone will be got rid of?

I have found no such wonderful secret. Nor do I expect to find it, nor do I expect that anyone else will ever find it. It is undiscovered. When you first began to read my words, perhaps there was a resurrection of hope in your breast. Perhaps you said to yourself, "This man will show me an easy, unfatiguing way of doing what I have so long in vain wished to do." Alas, no! The fact is that there is no easy way, no royal road. The path to Mecca is extremely hard and stony, and the worst of it is that you never quite get there after all.

The most important preliminary to the task of arranging one's life so that one may live fully and comfortably within one's daily budget of twenty-four hours is the calm realization of the extreme difficulty of the task, of the sacrifices and the endless effort which it demands. I cannot too strongly insist on this.

If you imagine that you will be able to achieve your ideal by ingeniously planning out a time-table with a pen on a piece of paper, you had better give up hope at once. If you are not prepared for discouragements and disillusions; if you will not be content with a small result for a big effort, then do not begin. Lie down again and resume the uneasy doze which you call your existence.

It is very sad, is it not, very depressing and

somber? And yet I think it is rather fine, too, this necessity for the tense bracing of the will before anything worth doing can be done. I rather like it myself. I feel it to be the chief thing that differentiates me from the cat by the fire.

"Well," you say, "assume that I am braced for battle. Assume that I have carefully weighed and comprehended your ponderous remarks; how do I begin?" Dear sir, or madam, you simply begin. There is no magic method of beginning. If a man standing on the edge of a swimming pool and wanting to jump into the cold water should ask you, "How do I begin to jump?" you would merely reply, "Just jump. Take hold of your nerves, and jump."

As I have previously said, the chief beauty about the constant supply of time is that you cannot waste it in advance. The next year, the next day, the next hour are lying ready for you, as perfect, as unspoiled, as if you had never wasted or misapplied a single moment in all your life. You can turn over a new leaf every hour if you choose. No object is served in waiting till next week or even until tomorrow. You may fancy that the water will be warmer next week. It won't. It will be colder.

Before you begin, let me murmur a few words

of warning in your ear. Beware of undertaking too much at the start. Be content with quite a little. Allow for accidents. Allow for human nature, especially your own.

A failure or so, in itself, would not matter, if it did not incur a loss of self-esteem and of self-confidence. But just as nothing succeeds like success, so nothing fails like failure. Most people who are ruined are ruined by attempting too much. Therefore, in setting out on the immense enterprise of living fully and comfortably within the narrow limits of twenty-four hours a day, let us avoid at any cost the risk of an early failure. I will not agree that, in this business at any rate, a glorious failure is better than a petty success. I am all for the petty success. A glorious failure leads to nothing; a petty success may lead to a success that is not petty.

So let us begin to examine the budget of the day's time. You say your day is already full to overflowing. How? How much time do you actually spend in earning your living? Seven hours perhaps, on the average? And in actual sleep, seven? I will add two hours and be generous. And I will defy you to account to me, on the spur of the moment, for the other eight hours!

In order to come to grips at once with the problem of time-spending, I must choose an individual case for examination. I can only deal with one case and that case cannot be the average case because there is no such case as the average case just as there is no such thing as an average person. Everyone is special.

However, if I take the case of someone who works in an office, whose office hours are from nine to five, and who spends fifty minutes morning and night in travelling between house and office, I shall have got as near to the average as facts permit. Certainly there are those who have to work longer hours for a living, but there are others who do not have to work so long.

Fortunately the financial side of existence does not interest us here. For our purpose the grocery clerk is exactly as well off as the millionaire. Now the great and profound mistake which my typical example makes in regard to his day is a mistake of general attitude, a mistake which impairs and weakens two-thirds of his energies and interests. In the majority of instances he does not precisely feel a passion for his work; at best he does not dislike it. He begins his daily work functions with reluctance, as late as he can, and he ends them with joy, as early as he can. And his engines while he is engaged in work are seldom at their full horsepower.

Yet, in spite of all this, he persists in looking upon those hours from nine to five as "the day," to which the nine hours preceding them and the seven hours following them are nothing but a prologue and epilogue. Such an attitude, unconscious though it be, of course kills his interest in the odd sixteen hours, with the result that, even if he does not waste them, he does not count them; he regards them simply as margin.

(This example could as well have been focused on a female rather than a male. Same results. S. P.)

This general attitude is utterly illogical and unhealthy, since it formally gives the central prominence to a patch of time and a bunch of activities which our one idea is to "get through" and have "done with." If we make two-thirds of our existence subservient to one-third, for which admittedly we have no absolutely feverish zest, how can we hope to live fully and completely? We cannot.

Important! If we wish to live fully and completely we must, in our mind, arrange a day within a day. And this inner day must begin at 5 P.M. and end at 9 A.M. It is a day of sixteen hours and during all those sixteen hours we have nothing whatever to do but cultivate our body and soul and our fellow men. During those sixteen hours we are free; we are not a wage-earner; we are not preoccupied by monetary cares. This must be our attitude. And our attitude is all important. Our success in life depends on it.

What? You say that full energy given to those sixteen hours will lessen the value of the eight hours at work? Not so. On the contrary, it will assuredly increase the value of the business eight. One of the chief things which my typical person has to learn is that the mental faculties are capable of continuous hard activity; they do not tire like an arm or a leg. All they want is change— not rest, except in sleep.

Let us study your average day. In justice to you I must say that you waste very little time before you leave the house in the morning at 8:10. In too many houses our hero or heroine arises at eight, breakfasts between 8:07 and 8:09$^1/_2$, and then bolts. But as soon as we slam the front door shut our mental faculties, which are tireless, become idle. We travel to work in a sort of mental coma, fighting traffic and humanity. Eventually you reach your place of work. And I abandon you there till five o'clock. I am aware that you have nominally an hour, at least, in the midst of the day, less than half of which time is given to eating. But I will leave you all that to spend as you choose.

I meet you again as you emerge from work. You are pale and tired. During the journey home you have been gradually working up the tired feeling. The tired feeling hangs heavy over the suburbs like a virtuous and melancholy cloud. You don't eat immediately on your arrival home. But in about an hour or so you feel as if you could sit up and take a little nourishment. And you do. Then you see friends, you play cards, you flirt with a book, you note that old age is creeping on, you take a stroll, you caress a piano.

(I cannot imagine how long Mr. Bennett's list of wasteful actions would be today with so many new attractions such as television and trips on the Internet to seduce us! S. P.)

Finally, it is quarter past eleven. Time to think about going to bed! At last you crawl under the blankets, exhausted by your day's work. Six hours, probably more, have vanished since you left work—gone like a dream, gone like magic, unaccountably gone!

This is a fairly simple case. But you say, "It's all very well for you to talk. However, one does get tired. One must see friends occasionally. One can't always be on the go." Just so. But when you arrange to go to the theatre what happens? You spare no toil in making yourself glorious in fine raiment and you go. Friends and fatigue have equally been forgotten, and the evening has seemed so exquisitely long. Can you deny that when you have something definite to look forward to at eventide, something that is to employ all your energy—the thought of that something gives a glow and a more intense vitality to the entire day?

What I suggest is that at six o'clock you look facts in the face and admit that you are not tired, because you are not, you know, and that you arrange your evening so that it is not cut in the middle by a meal. Dine earlier in the evening. By so doing you will have a clear expanse of at least three hours. I do not suggest that you should employ three hours every night of your life in using up your mental energy. But I do suggest that you might, for a commencement, employ an hour and a half every other evening in some important and consecutive cultivation of the mind. You will still be left with three evenings for friends, bridge, tennis, domestic scenes, odd reading, pipes, gardening, pottering, and prize competitions. You will also still have that terrific wealth of sixty-nine hours between 5 P.M. on Friday and 9 A.M. on Monday. If you persevere you will soon want to pass four evenings, and perhaps five, in some sustained endeavor to be genuinely alive. And you will fall out of that habit of muttering to yourself at 11:15 P.M., "Time to be thinking about going to bed." The person who begins to go to bed forty minutes before opening the bedroom door is bored; that is to say, he or she is not living.

But remember, at the start, those ninety nocturnal minutes thrice a week must be the most important minutes in the ten thousand and eighty of the week. And having once decided to achieve a certain task, achieve it at all costs of tedium and distaste. The gain in self-confidence of having accomplished a tiresome labor is immense.

Finally, in choosing the first occupations of those evening hours, be guided by nothing whatever but your taste and natural inclination. It is a fine thing to be a walking encyclopedia of philosophy, but if you happen to have no liking for philosophy, and to have a liking for the natural history of street-cries, much better to leave philosophy alone and take to street-cries.

(Make the time, each day, to search for opportunities right where you are now and enjoy the miracles that will soon take place in your life! S. P.)

X

THE FOURTH RUNG OF LIFE'S LADDER

*S*everal decades before Norman Vincent Peale was writing and talking about "the power of positive thinking" and W. Clement Stone was promoting the benefits of a "positive mental attitude," a brilliant man named Albert Lewis Pelton, in a book entitled *The Creed of the Conquering Chief*, was teaching the nation how to deal with failure and achieve astounding success through the use of their mental powers.

In his tiny but powerful volume, Pelton carefully explained a code of thought and conduct, based on natural law, necessary for one to rise above the masses and achieve the great status of success common to all leaders or "chiefs."

Ponder well and long the wise suggestions that follow. Learn to apply them in your daily activities and you will achieve goals you never dreamed possible. S. P.)

For many years I have been an investigator in the field of phenomena known as psychology—the study of the human mind. Our minds have two levels, the conscious and the subconscious. The mind-life of which we are aware, in our daily duties, is the conscious phase. However, deep down below the surface there exists a vast mental life of which we are not aware, the subconscious realm, containing a powerful reservoir of thought-energy.

This special reservoir is constantly receiving supplies of thought material from the upper mind, storing, combining, mixing, and multiplying it all into a potential mass of energy for those who have learned the secret of tapping this powerful source.

Behold! This special message is for you if you have a burning desire to improve the conditions of your life. I call you fearlessly to look upon the inner shrine wherein you hold dear your ambition of ambitions—that guarded secret which is nothing less than your desire to succeed, to be supreme in your daily efforts. In short, it is yourself calling for conquest.

Accompany me with an open mind and the spirit of investigation. Pay close attention to my words. I am to speak to you of *The Creed of the Conquering Chief*.

There is nothing novel or new in the idea of conquest. From the moment you first call your vital powers into action in a gasp for breath at birth, on through the years until you again gasp for breath before passing into the next state of being, you are confronted with the constant necessity of conquest. It is instinctive and incessant.

Before going any further it is important that you have a clear understanding of the exact meaning of this subject. Note these definitions:

Creed—a summary of what is believed
Conquering—the act of subduing or overcoming by mental power in order to achieve success
Chief—a truly successful individual, prominent in any quality or undertaking

The Creed of the Conquering Chief, therefore, is an investigation into the art of achieving success through our mental powers and gaining the Great Victory through definite and important liens of human conduct until one is a leader, a chief.

The price that every conquering chief must pay for prominence is the envy and jealousy and attack by the hordes lower down. It calls for a masterful brain and nerve and manner to stay there—at the forefront.

Few people can maintain the stamina necessary for the perilous position of leadership and success. It is the high art of conquest. Let me show you the way but if you are to go on with me you must have an open mind. Resolve to be swayed neither by feeling, sentiment nor guesswork but always seek to discover the underlying law and act upon that.

Mankind has existed for thousands of years but never have we succeeded in defeating the action of natural law. To achieve success, to become a conquering chief, you must realize that there is a natural rule of action, a definite cause, preceding every desired result. You know that if you turn a railroad switch a certain way it will throw the oncoming express into a siding—and wreck it. You know that if you put your finger into the fire it will be burned. You know that if you jump off a high building down to the pavement, your bones will be broken.

These are mechanical and physical laws. They have always existed. Mankind gradually learns what they are and then uses them to make life easier. The possibility of wireless telegraphy existed ten thousand years ago, as it does now, but we did not then know the law. Nor did we know how to use it to achieve productive results.

I want you to consider this analogy of cause and effect as it applies to *The Creed of the Conquering Chief*—to your success in general.

Right at this moment you are confronted by problems which you want to solve to your best advantage. You want success. You want ability. You want money. You want influence. You want promotion. You want a hundred and one things. If you will begin, today, to investigate, observe, test, analyze and endeavor to discover what is the Law that will yield the results you want you can find that Law. Put it into operation and victory will be yours.

I cannot go into the details of using this Law in any particular way you wish to use it. I can only give you the principle. It is for you, in your own individual way, to discover the details and put them into action. Knowing the scientific method of thinking and using the natural Law are the first essentials of achieving success.

Before the advent of steam railways, electric transportation, flying machines, automobiles and ocean liners the average person was supposed to be familiar with conditions approximately 15 miles from home. Heed my words and soon you will be free of the 15-mile type of mind. Demand the thousand-mile radius—the Open Mind.

Grasp this important fact. You have within your makeup, right now, every one of the qualities and traits which the great person has. The degree to which you develop and apply these forces is to a very great extent one of your own choosing. Remember that to falter, hesitate, and back down on your plans—to give up—to weaken and lazily quit, is to destroy the power of conquest within you. Make great plans and forever fight forward for their consummation. However, at first make plans that are well within your power of accomplishment. Do them. Surmount them. When you have risen a degree, gradually brave steeper ascents. Try the larger task. Go upwards. Dominate. Conquer, until you reach and master the big things.

All day long you are searching for power. You

want power to succeed; you want power to do and to dare; you want power to deal with others; you strive for power to rise above the commonplaces of life—to be a leader. It is here that I want to introduce another element of our Creed as follows:

<u>All the Power you can ever use now exists and awaits your intelligent mastery.</u>

To recognize those forces which now exist is very difficult for the mass of men and women. It is so easy, so entrancing, so beautiful to let the mind roam off into the Elysian fields of dreams, of idealism; to shut our eyes to that which actually exists—the conditions in which we are really placed. We may shut ourselves in a closet and vow there is no such thing as sunshine. And yet it exists just the same.

We humans are not equal—never have been—and never will be. So long as ambition enters into the measure of a person and free will exists, there will be leaders and followers. There will be the great and the small. Socialism, Utopias, and any other plans to make all of us equal will never stand the test of time. Suppose two men to be equals at night, and the one rises at six while the other sleeps until nine the next morning—what becomes of your levelling? Nature secures advance, not by the reduction of all to a common level but by the encouragement and conservation of what is best.

The mammoth chrysanthemum is the result of cutting away from the plant all other buds and shoots and flooding the whole plant's life force into the one magnificent bloom.

I believe in this as applied to the individual. I believe in eliminating surrounding clods and weeds and worthless material. Aim higher than the others. Get out of the crowd! This is the law of the Conquering Chief.

(Have you ever stood in front of your bathroom mirror and talked to yourself? Consider these words you are reading as the advice being offered to you by that image in the mirror. Your progress as an individual is always a matter of inner unfoldment. Life moves from within, outward. The germ or vitality is always at the center, not on the surface. The growth of the tree or the plant, of the animal or the fruit, is not that of adding on the outside, but a supply from the inside. You are now beginning to understand the powerful message contained on this rung of your ladder as you slowly come to realize that you will determine your own position in life according to the amount of intelligent effort you exert. S. P.)

Personal life has improved through the ages,

ever acquiring more control and extending the individual's reach to a widening sphere of mastery. First it was over other creatures; then it was the elements; then it was travel and navigation—the crossing of a continent—the sending of messages with or without mechanical connections; the conquest of the air, etc.

And now there is still another goal to be reached—the sending of thought from mind to mind, without any intervening physical agent. We now live in the great Age of Mind—an era when mental forces reign supreme.

The great successes of today—the modern conquering chiefs—are those with great mind power. From this we may draw a brief rule for our Creed as follows:

Mind power is today the sole measure of mastery. Resolve that your own brain shall be made to work for you with all its might.

Always strive to be greater than you are. You must surpass yourself. In each successive act, test, encounter, thought, try to be greater than in the one previous. You are what you are now but in an hour you must be more than you are now. In every action you take, exert more power to surpass yourself.

You and I are architects of the minutes. We

build ourselves every moment. What you are this minute is the result of what you were building during the thousands of minutes that have already passed. What you will be in a minute from now depends upon what you are now, plus—what you are mentally demanding that this present moment shall add. With every turnaround of the clock's second hand are you building yourself anew—are you changing, altering, revising, remaking, increasing?

Just as surely as the pilot of a vessel deliberately moves his wheel one way, and swings the huge ship to the east—or moves it the other way and swings it toward the setting sun, and so pursues his course as he elects, and finally reaches his port if his steering has been correct—<u>just so can you deliberately direct your own course toward any goal.</u>

I repeat: You are the product of minutes. Each minute is an opportunity to build—for growth, advance, gain, supremacy, and *conquest.*

It all rests with you.

Keep your eyes on the minutes.

The minutes make the man or woman.

I have observed, through a lifetime of study, that all of us can be divided into three main classes.

1. Those with *willpower* (the leaders).

2. Those with *desire* (whose intentions are good but who fail to put forth the necessary dominance and action to win out. They are the ones who wish instead of demand).

3. Those men and women of *fate* (who give up all the glory of human achievement because they say "it's all no use—things will never come my way." This remark is correct. They certainly will never "come" but they can be *appropriated* and that is what those with willpower will do).

The Conquering Chief naturally belongs to the first class—the dynamic personality asserting its own, claiming its own and invariably striving to take the action necessary to achieve victory.

Look to the biography of the world's great, living or dead, and in nearly every instance one masterful trait stands out more prominent than all others. It is the real secret of their supremacy. And this I term indomitable, unconquerable *Will*— <u>self-declared refusal to yield an inch to the external forces which seek to thwart progress.</u>

Napoleon was a superlative example of it; Bismarck had it; Grant illustrated it splendidly; Morgan mastered it; Roosevelt in action was a whirlwind example of it; Edison owes his fam-

ous concentration and persistence to it. Yes—
the captains of Industry. Finance, Invention, Art,
Science—all build their immortal achievements
upon the invincible power of Will.

"I will" is the sovereign state of mind—the
most intense attitude of self toward all external
forces. Your *Self* with *Will* in action has for servants the body, intellect, and the feelings. And
with those servants fully disciplined you can conquer the world, the universe.

Read the following pledge, again and again:

*Knowing that only as I enter the ranks of the first
grade of humans . . . those of willpower . . . can I expect
to be a conquering chief, I do pledge myself to the large
development of this prime quality. I will neither passively
wish for things, nor drop back to the third grade of those
who abdicate their realms under the delusion that life is
a matter of prearranged destiny.*

Ask no one for permission to perform that
which is within you to do. Boldly strike out upon
your own initiative and *do* while the multitude
stand by in mouth-stretched awe. The reliant, the
bold—the Conquering Chief steps forward and
plucks the prize while all the others stand by and
marvel at his daring.

"The greatest successes have been for those

who have accepted the heaviest risks." Mull that over for some time. It is a way of life for the Conquering Chief. The world is filled with cowards who dare not attempt big things. Convention and ridicule and "what will people say?" are ghosts which take the starch from them. Forget these bugaboos. Kick them into the scrap heap. The best successes are open to you if only you take the heaviest risks, balanced by cool, discerning judgment.

"Dare what no one else will dare. <u>Seek to accomplish what no one else will attempt.</u> There is no better way to display yourself as a superior being in your own and in others' eyes."

Oh, I confess that I am not advancing a philosophy and creed for the mass of humanity. Here and there is a man or woman who will gather together the threads of my sentences and weave for himself or herself a wonderful fabric.

I believe in that individual.

I believe in that person who works out his or her own destiny on a grand scale.

My idea of strength is the rugged oak on the mountain peak. Stalwart and sturdy, growing and existing against the odds of nature. The price for this prominence among men and women is the struggle to tower above belittlement, insult, jeer, sarcasm and insolence.

Can *you* pay that price?

Will you pay that price?

XI

✦

THE FIFTH RUNG OF
LIFE'S LADDER

"*L*ife to each of us is an ever-changing panorama. The sights of yesterday are old, the scenes of today are swiftly passing, and the pictures of tomorrow will be new. Each day comes freighted with greater opportunities and enlarged interests. The great problem of the ages and the burning question of today is how to succeed. Every generation of the past has been confronted by this problem and each individual is today asking the same vital question. The hopes and hearts of all men and women are alike. Your hopes are like mine. I wish for happiness. So do you. I desire to succeed. So do you. Our ideals of happiness or success may differ but each is striving for that ideal we call success. No person in his or her right mind ever wished for ruin and failure and grief.

"Many a man and woman would do better than they are now doing if they only knew how. This book, *Portraits and Principles*, was created for them. While its writers cannot travel the road of life for you and so give that perfect knowledge that can only be had by actual experience, yet next to that actual experience the most important thing in undertaking an unknown journey is a good guidebook.

"I have been fortunate to gather together, in this book, some thoughts and suggestions about success and life from the wisest minds I know. Listen to their counsel and kindly words of advice. It may save you much heartache and despair hereafter. You, too, would succeed. It is not natural to wish to be a wreck, to be counted as 'thorns' or 'chaff.' So it is safe to assume that you want to make your life a blessing to yourself and others. It is well, then, to remember that there is no teacher like experience, nor any lessons so impressive and so costly as hers.

"Very many, indeed, will learn at no other school, and all of us have, at some time, to take more or less lessons there. Yet it is neither wise nor safe to depend entirely on what you may learn from her for you will find that the knowledge gained there, however valuable, often comes too late to be of benefit to you in this life and serves only to remind you of previous mistakes. Be willing, therefore, to learn from others."

(These words were written by the head of America's largest publishing house of the last century, William C. King. Because of his position he was able to convince some of the wisest minds of his time to contribute their thoughts on success for his own book, *Portraits and Principles*, which became one of the first bestsellers based on the achievement of success. The advice you are about to read is old, but priceless, and if heeded will save you countless heartaches. S. P.)

Singleness of Aim. Success is a relative term and varies in its meaning with the nature of one's business in life. In a battle, to win a victory over the foe is success. If you start out on a journey, to reach the point of destination is success. The physician who saves his patients, the lawyer who wins his case, the political leader who obtains office, the merchant who makes a profit, the manufacturer who widens commerce, the man of science who enlarges the sum of human knowledge, each, in his own sphere reaches a success that is relatively complete.

Having chosen your occupation, you, of course, wish to succeed in it. How can you best do so? <u>By concentration of your efforts upon a single thing.</u> Many persons spread their energies over too wide a field with the result that while they might succeed handsomely in one venture, by undertaking too many they dissipate their powers of supervision as well as capital and in the end fail to obtain their hoped-for success. You should always mass your force at that part of the line where the brunt of the battle is to come. If you have decided to win success in that particular business, stay there and conquer. Many people can make a grand success of one particular thing but they cannot win in a dozen different undertakings.

False Standards. Success! What is this thing that all desire, few comprehend, and less are willing to pay for? Many think the coveted prize will fall to them without effort, but it will not. If it were something external, it might be so. Possibly we could then wander aimlessly, drifting with the tide, shifting with every changing breeze and gather success as a sort of side issue while lounging along the highway of life. But it cannot be so acquired; it is not for sale upon those terms; it is not accident, but a result; it does not come by chance but as a reward of long and painful effort.

Success in its highest expression is making the best of one's self; it is doing with steadfast, unremitting fidelity the homely duties of everyday life; it follows closely upon an unwavering recognition of the fact that the surest guarantee of advancement is the faithful discharge of the duties of the lower place and filling the subordinate position so full of honest service that in the nature of things promotion must ensue. It was the person faithful over a few things who was made a ruler over many. <u>In a word, success is character.</u> Make the best of your talents, your opportunities, yourself. Beware of false standards in your conduct and methods of life. Imitate not those whose moral lives have the slightest taint either by associations or personal conduct. Follow not the example of anyone whose methods of business are at all questionable. Keep your life and character free from blemish or stain. Aim high. Low motives, inferior aspirations, any attainment less than the best you are capable of are all unworthy of you.

Waiting for Something to Turn Up. There is a proverb, long current, that "God takes care of the lame and lazy." I suspect it originated in the philosophy of those who are always "waiting for something to turn up." Of course these people are always disappointed. They deserve to be. They come to nothing but disaster and disgrace. Things do not "turn up" in this world. They are turned up. There is an endless chain of efficient, natural causes running through life. Nothing comes from nothing. Multiply even billions by a zero and zero is the product. There is also a law of equity. We all get what we deserve. Victory is won only by strenuous, brave battle. Success is gained only by effort, by labor, by self-denial, by skill and patient long-continued struggle. "Waiting for something to turn up" is waiting for moonbeams to turn into silver, for magic and chance to take the place of natural law in the universe.

But perhaps you may ask, "Are there then no favoring circumstances and conditions in life? Is there no tide in the affairs of men which taken at its flood leads on to fortune?" Yes, doubtless; but only for those who work and wait, not for those who lie idle and wait. They are for those who are out in the midst of life's activities, "doing their level best" under all conditions and circumstances, not for those who skulk and shirk. The best chances come only to those who take all the chances, good and bad, and make the most of them. The big fish, as well as the little, are caught by those who go a-fishing, not by those who stay at home.

Eyes That See. As I write, my eyes take in the paper before me, then the various objects in the room, in their form, color, direction, and distance. I next look from my window and see the dwellings, factories, business blocks, and church spires, and the hills stretching far away into the dim distance, while the clouds, like phantom ships, go sailing in a sea of blue. All these things I take knowledge of by means of a little spherical mechanism less than an inch in diameter. The objects on my desk I may touch and handle; the faraway hills I also touch, though not with my hand. I cannot go to them except by a journey of many hours but I open my eyes and they are brought to me on wings of light.

So many of us go through life with open eyes indeed, but with a brain behind the eye so sluggish that we see little more than does the small dog by our side. The eye is, after all, an instrument of the brain, and what we urge is that the brain be taught to use, with more skill, this delicate mechanism. We need educated eyes, trained powers of perception and reproduction. Walk through the streets of the city with a companion, look at the same store window for an instant and then ascertain which can give the fuller account of what was seen. The eye is capable of being trained to a process of instantaneous photography which will afford both pleasure and profit to the possessor.

The difference between the success of this one and the failure of that one is often simply in the use of the eyes. One sees and seizes that at which the other but idly glances. The successful person indeed sees more than the facts or objects which come under his notice. He sees them as doors of opportunity which wait to be pushed open and give him access to something better beyond. In reading the lives of inventors and discoverers we often come to the expression, "He noticed that—" and then follows the account of how some commonplace thing, which others had repeatedly passed around or stumbled over, became his stepping stone to success.

Discoveries and inventions are rarely the result of chance. Discoverers and inventors "notice" because they have cultivated their powers of observation, they have eyes that see. Sir Isaac Newton worked out the statement of the law of gravitation and discovered that the same force that caused the apple to fall from the tree in his mother's orchard kept the moon in its orbit. Others had seen apples fall and the moon move onward in the heavens but he was the first to see the connection between them.

For true success there must be not only the general powers of observation but a specialized training of those powers so that you will always be searching for your specialty. Yonder stand three men on a hilltop. The first is a dealer in real estate. His trained eye enables him to estimate the fertility of those broad acres in the valley and the value of those forest-covered slopes or the possibilities of making the sightly eminence upon which they stand a suburban settlement where homes may be built away from the noise and smoke of the city. The next is a geologist. His eyes take in the nature of the soil, the rock formations, the outlines of hills and valleys and courses of rivers and he sees how, through unmeasured ages, the forces of nature have been bringing to its present form the region of country which is spread out at his feet. The third is a painter. For the possibilities and utilities of the valleys and hillsides, or the processes by which they came to their present form he cares but little. He looks with an artist's eye and his soul swells with an artist's joy and he longs to capture for his canvas those valleys of verdure, the river which like a silver ribbon winds among the green, the wooded hills, the white houses away up the valley and the hazy sky. Each of these individuals has eyes that see but the eyes of each have been differently trained and so each sees his specialty.

Your eyes are the windows to your future. Use them well and they will lead you straight to the good life you deserve.

Practice Secures Perfection. There is only one way to learn how to do a thing and that is by doing it. No art, no pursuit requiring skill, is mastered at once. It must be wrestled with long and patiently before it gives up its secret.

One can perhaps learn how to saw wood in about an hour and then earn wages at that business for the rest of his life. It is a useful occupation but demands neither skill nor long training for its successful prosecution. Muscle with a moderate degree of intelligence is all that is necessary.

It is very different with pursuits demanding dexterity, skill, and brains. Years are required to gain mastery over them. "How long did it take you to prepare that sermon?" asked someone of Dr. Lyman Beecher. "Forty years" was his prompt reply. Giardini, when asked how long it would take to learn the violin, replied, "Twelve hours a day for twenty years." It would be very pleasant if we could learn to play the violin or piano by inspiration. But the great musicians did not learn in that way. Incessant practice was the price they paid for their proficiency. Not by sudden inspiration but by painstaking cultivation are dexterity, mastership, and facile power of any kind acquired. Nothing is done easily, not even walking or talking, that was not done with difficulty at first. Practice in any line of action brings to our aid the law of habit, a law which reigns in the muscular and mental no less than in the moral realms of action.

Do anything a sufficient number of times and you acquire facility in doing it. Every action tends to repeat itself; repeated action begets habit and habit is second nature. All the powers and possibilities within us are subject to this powerful law of habit. Practice puts the law into operation, arouses latent possibilities and calls into action powers which would otherwise have lain ingloriously dormant.

Listen to a great pianist like Paderewski, whose touch is marvelous, whose fingers glide over the keys as if in instinct with life, and it seems as though it must always have been easy for him to play; but on inquiry you learn that it was by practice, incessant and severe, from early years to manhood, that he acquired that exquisite skill.

Even Titian and Raphael had to begin by drawing straight lines; Beethoven and Mozart by picking out the notes one by one; and Shakespeare himself had to learn the alphabet before he wrote *Hamlet* and *King Lear*. Little by little these things are learned. "There is no such thing," said Daniel Webster, "as extemporaneous acquisition. Perfection is not gained any more than heaven at a single bound. We build the ladder by which we rise."

(Remember those wise words as you climb this, your own special ladder of life, which will, rung by rung, increase your value as you absorb each wise old book's ration of wisdom until its suggested actions become an important part of your daily routine. S. P.)

Be not discouraged if progress seems slow. Time and toil will work wonders. Practice is the prelude to the song of victory. Do your best every time. Remember Beethoven's words, "The barriers are not erected which say to aspiring talents and industry, 'thus far and no farther.' "

The Importance of Courtesy. Your manners generally indicate your character. They are an index of your tastes, feelings, and temper and usually reveal the kind of company you have been accustomed to keep.

There is a kind of conventional manner, a superficial veneer, a "society cloak," used by some people on special occasions which is of little importance, no practical value, and as transparent as it is worthless. Artificial politeness is an attempt to deceive, an effort to make others believe that we are what we are not; while true politeness is the outward expression of the natural character, the external sins of the internal being. Thus a beautiful character reflects a beautiful manner.

There is a vast difference between "society customs" and genuine good manners. The former is a bold but fruitless attempt to counterfeit a noble virtue while the latter is the natural expression of a heart filled with honest intentions.

True politeness must be born of sincerity. It must be the response of the heart otherwise it makes no lasting impression, for no amount of "posture" and "surface polish" can be substituted for honesty and truthfulness.

The genius of a person may for a time hide many defects, but the natural character cannot long be hidden from view; the real individual is sooner or later bound to come to the surface, revealing imperfections, natural tendencies, and personal characteristics.

Good manners are developed through a spirit imbued with unselfishness, kindness, justness, and generosity. A person possessed of these qualities will be found gentle and polite. Good manners should be essential factors in our education and cannot be too strongly emphasized when we realize that they are but the outward expression of inward virtues, and like the hands of a watch indicate that the machinery within is perfect and true.

Among the qualities which contribute to worldly success, true politeness takes first rank. Especially in the business world it is our bearing towards others that often, more than any other circumstance, promotes or obstructs our advancement and success in life.

How courteous we are to others generally determines our success or failure. The person whose heart and life are right will exhibit those winning qualities so universally admired and will secure good will and hearty support of both friend and stranger. There is no field of labor where good manners are out of place. Pleasing manners constitute one of our golden keys which turn the bolts of the door leading to success and happiness.

XII

~~~~~

THE SIXTH RUNG OF
LIFE'S LADDER

"*The* aphorism, 'As a man thinketh in his heart so is he,' not only embraces the whole of man's being, but is so comprehensive as to reach out to every condition and circumstance of his life. A man is literally what he thinks, his character being the complete sum of all his thoughts."

(James Allen wrote those wise words more than a hundred years ago and his tiny book from which they were taken, *As A Man Thinketh*, has been hailed by countless generations as one of the most powerful and relevant guidelines to a good life ever delivered to the inhabitants of this earth. There is only one hurdle to Allen's invaluable advice for the truth-seeker of today and that is his constant reference to humanity in general as "man," a common custom of his time. I have labored long to convert the brilliant author's words to the first person without altering his meaning in any way so that as you read each solemn declaration for a better life they will apply to you whether you are male or female. No one has dared to tamper with these powerful words for more than a century . . . until now. S. P.)

The wise saying, "As I think in my heart so I am" not only embraces the whole of my being, but is so comprehensive as to reach out to every condition and circumstance of my life. I am literally *what I think*, my character being the complete sum of all my thoughts.

As the plant springs from, and could not be without, the seed, so every act of mine springs from the hidden seeds of my thoughts and could not have appeared without them. This applies just as well to those acts called "spontaneous" and "unpremeditated" as to those which are deliberately executed.

I am made or unmade by myself; in the armory of thought I forge the weapons by which I destroy myself; I also fashion the tools with which I can build for myself heavenly mansions of joy and strength and peace. By the right choice and true application of thought I am able to ascend to Divine Perfection; by the abuse and wrong application of thought, I descend below the level of the beast. Between these two extremes are all the grades of character, and I am their maker and master.

Of all the beautiful truths pertaining to the soul which have been restored and brought to light in this age, none is more gladdening or fruitful of divine promise and confidence than this—that I am the master of thought, the moulder of character, and the maker and shaper of my condition, my environment, and my destiny.

As a being of Power, Intelligence, and Love, and the creator of my own thoughts, I hold the key to every situation, and possess within myself that transforming and regenerative agency by which I may make myself whatever I will.

I am always the master, even in my weakest and most abandoned state; but in my weakness and degradation I am the foolish master who misgoverns my "household." When I begin to reflect upon my condition, and to search diligently for the Law upon which my being is established, I then become wise, I then commence directing my energies with intelligence, and fashioning my thoughts to fruitful issues.

Only by much searching and mining are gold and diamonds obtained, and I can find every truth connected with my being if I will dig deep into the mine of my soul.

My mind may be likened to a garden, which may be intelligently cultivated or allowed to run wild; but whether cultivated or neglected, it must, and will, *bring forth*. If no useful seeds are put into it, then an abundance of useless weed-seeds will *fall* therein, and will continue to produce their kind.

Just as a gardener cultivates his plot, keeping it free from weeds, and growing the flowers and fruits which he requires, so may I tend the garden of my mind, weeding out all the wrong, useless, and impure thoughts, and cultivating toward perfection the flowers and fruits of right, useful, and pure thoughts. By pursuing this process, I will soon discover that I am the master-gardener of my soul, the director of my life.

I will only be buffeted by circumstances so long as I believe myself to be the creature of outside conditions. When I realize that I am a creative power and that I may command the hidden soil and seeds of my being out of which circumstances grow, I then become the rightful master of myself.

Every thought-seed sown or allowed to fall into the mind, and to take root there, produces its own, blossoming sooner or later into action and bearing its own harvest of opportunity and circumstance. Good thoughts bear good fruit, bad thoughts bad fruit.

The outer world of circumstance shapes itself to the inner world of thought, and both pleasant and unpleasant outside conditions are factors which make for the ultimate good of the individual. As the reaper of my own harvest, I learn both by suffering and bliss.

I do not attract that which I want, but that which I am. My whims, fancies, and ambitions are thwarted at every step, but my inmost thoughts and desires are fed with their own food, be it foul or clean. The "divinity that shapes our ends" is in myself; it is my very self!

Good thoughts and actions can never produce bad results; bad thoughts and actions can never produce good results. This is but saying that nothing can come from corn but corn, nothing from nettles but nettles. We all understand this law in the natural world and work with it; but few understand it in the mental and moral world (though its operation there is just as simple and undeviating), and we, therefore, do not cooperate with it.

Suffering is *always* the effect of wrong thought in some direction. It is an indication that I am out of harmony with myself. The sole and supreme use of suffering is to purify, to burn out all that is useless and impure. Suffering ceases for me when I am pure.

As I commence to alter my thoughts towards things and other people, things and other people will alter towards me.

The proof of this truth is in every person, and it therefore admits of easy investigation by systematic introspection and self-analysis. When I radically alter my thoughts, I will be astonished at the rapid transformation it will effect in the material conditions of my life. Thought cannot be kept secret. It rapidly crystallizes into habit, and habit solidifies into circumstance. Thoughts of fear, doubt, and indecision solidify into failure and slavish dependence while thoughts of courage and self-reliance crystallize into success and plenty.

A particular train of thought persisted in, be it good or bad, cannot fail to produce its results on the character and circumstances. I cannot directly choose my circumstances, but I can choose my thoughts and so indirectly, yet surely, shape my circumstances.

Let me cease my negative thinking and all the world will soften towards me and be ready to help me. Let me put away my weakly and sickly thoughts and opportunities will spring up on every hand to aid my strong resolves. Let me encourage good thoughts, and no hard fate will bind me down to wretchedness and shame. The world is my kaleidoscope, and the varying combinations of colors which at every succeeding moment it presents to me are the exquisitely adjusted pictures of my ever moving thoughts.

My body is the servant of my mind. It obeys the operations of the mind, whether they be deliberately chosen or automatically expressed. At the bidding of unlawful thoughts my body sinks rapidly into disease and decay. At the command of glad and beautiful thoughts it becomes clothed with youthfulness and beauty.

Disease and health, like circumstances, are rooted in thought. Sickly thoughts will express themselves through a sickly body. Thoughts of fear have been known to kill a man as speedily as a bullet, and they are continually killing thousands of people just as surely though less rapidly. The people who live in fear of disease are the people who get it. Anxiety quickly demoralizes the whole body, and lays it open to the entrance of disease, while impure thoughts, even if not physically indulged, will soon shatter the nervous system.

Thought is the fount of action, life, and manifestation. If I make the fountain pure, all will be pure.

Change of diet will not help me if I do not change my thoughts. When I make my thoughts pure, I no longer desire impure food.

Clean thoughts make clean habits. The so-called saint who does not wash his body is not a saint. He who has strengthened and purified his thoughts does not need to consider the malevolent microbe.

If I am to perfect my body, I must guard my mind. If I am to renew my body, I must beautify my mind. Thoughts of malice, envy, disappointment, and despondency will rob my body of its health and grace. A sour face does not come by chance; it is made by sour thoughts. Wrinkles that mar are drawn by folly, passion, pride.

As I cannot have a sweet and wholesome abode unless I admit the air and sunshine freely into my rooms, so a strong body and a bright, happy, or serene countenance can only result from the free admittance into my mind of thoughts of joy and goodwill and serenity.

There is no physician like cheerful thought for dissipating the ills of the body. There is no comforter to compare with goodwill for dispersing the shadows of grief and sorrow. To live continually in thoughts of ill will, cynicism, suspicion, and envy is to be confined in a self-made prison-hole. But to think well of all, to be cheerful with all, to patiently learn to find the good in all—such unselfish thoughts are the very portals of heaven; and to dwell day by day in thoughts of peace toward every creature will bring abounding peace to their possessor.

Until thought is linked with purpose there is no intelligent accomplishment. With the majority the bark of thought is allowed to "drift" upon the ocean of life. Aimlessness is a vice, and such drifting must not continue for me if I am to steer clear of catastrophe and destruction.

If I have no central purpose in my life I can fall an easy prey to petty worries, fears, troubles, and self-pity, all of which are indications of weakness, which lead, just as surely as deliberately planned sins, to failure, unhappiness, and loss.

I must conceive of a legitimate purpose in my

heart and set out to accomplish it. I should make this purpose the centralizing point of my thoughts. It may take the form of a spiritual ideal or it may be a worldly object according to my nature at the time but, whichever it is, I should steadily focus my thoughts upon the object which I have set before myself. I should make this purpose my supreme duty and completely devote myself to its attainment, not allowing my thoughts to wander away into ephemeral fancies, longings, and imaginings. This is the royal road to self-control and true concentration of thought.

Even if I fail again and again to accomplish my purpose (as I might until weakness is overcome), *the strength of character I gain* will be the measure of my *true* success, and this will form a new starting point for future power and triumph.

Those who are not prepared for the accomplishment of a *great* purpose should fix their thoughts upon the faultless performance of their duty, no matter how insignificant their task may appear. Only in this way can their thoughts be gathered and focussed, and resolution and energy be developed, which being done, there is nothing which may not be accomplished.

To put away aimlessness and weakness, and to begin to think with purpose, is to enter the ranks of those strong ones who only recognize failure as one of the pathways to attainment; who make all conditions serve them, and who think strongly, attempt fearlessly, and accomplish masterfully.

When I set goals for myself I will mentally mark out a *straight* pathway to their achievement, looking neither to the right nor the left. Doubts and fears will be rigorously excluded; they are disintegrating elements which break up the straight line of effort, rendering it crooked, ineffectual, useless. Thoughts of doubt and fear never accomplish anything, and never can. They always lead to failure.

When I have conquered doubt and fear I have conquered failure. My every thought will be allied with power, and all difficulties will be bravely met and wisely overcome.

All that I achieve and all that I fail to achieve is the direct result of my own thoughts. My weakness and strength, purity and impurity, are my own, and not another's; they are brought about by myself, and not by another; and they can only be altered by me, never by another. My condition is also my own and my suffering as well as my happiness are all evolved from within. As I think, so I am; as I continue to think, so I remain.

A strong person cannot help a weaker unless

that weaker is *willing* to be helped. I must, through my own efforts, develop the strength which I admire in others. No one but myself can change my condition. I can only rise, conquer, and achieve by lifting up my thoughts. I can only remain weak, and abject, and miserable by refusing to lift up my thoughts.

There is no progress, no achievement without sacrifice, and my worldly success will depend on how much I fix my mind on the development of my plans, and the strengthening of my resolution and self-reliance. And the higher I lift my thoughts the greater will be my success and the more blessed and enduring will be my achievements.

Victories attained by right thought can only be maintained by watchfulness. Many give way when success is assured, and rapidly fall back into failure. To accomplish little I need only sacrifice little; to achieve much I must sacrifice much; to reach great heights I must sacrifice greatly.

If I cherish a beautiful vision, a lofty ideal in my heart, I will one day realize it. Columbus cherished a vision of another world and he discovered it; Copernicus fostered the vision of a multiplicity of worlds and a wider universe, and he revealed it; Buddha beheld the vision of a spiritual world of stainless beauty and perfect peace, and he entered it.

I will cherish my visions; cherish my ideals; cherish the music that stirs in my heart, the beauty that forms in my mind, for out of them will grow all delightful conditions, all heavenly environment and of these, if I remain true to them, my world will at last be built.

I will dream lofty dreams, and as I dream, so I become. My Vision is the promise of what I shall be one day, my Ideal is the prophecy of what I shall at last unveil.

The greatest achievement was at first and for a time a dream. The oak sleeps in the acorn; the bird waits in the egg; and in the highest vision of the soul a waking angel stirs. Dreams are the seedlings of realities.

My current circumstances may seem difficult and hopeless but they will not long remain so if I but perceive an Ideal and strive to reach it. I cannot travel *within* and stand still *without*. Now I understand that I will realize the Vision of my heart, be it base or beautiful, or a mixture of both, for I will always gravitate toward that which I, secretly, most love. Into my hands will be placed the exact results of my own thoughts; I will receive that which I earn; no more, no less. Whatever my present environment may be, I will fall, remain, or rise with my thoughts, my Vision, my Ideal. I will become as small as my controlling desire; as great as my dominant aspiration.

The thoughtless, the ignorant, and the indolent, seeing only the apparent effects of things and not the things themselves, talk of luck, of fortune, and chance. Seeing a man grow rich, they say, "How lucky he is!" Observing another become intellectual, they exclaim, "How highly favored he is!" And noting the saintly character and wide influence of another, they remark, "How chance aids him at every turn!" They do not see the trials and failures and struggles which these people have voluntarily encountered in order to gain their experience. They have no knowledge of the sacrifices which were made in order to gain experience, no knowledge of the sacrifices made or the efforts put forth, so that the insurmountable was overcome.

In all human affairs there are *efforts*, and there are *results*, and the strength of the effort is the measure of the result. Chance is not. "Gifts," powers, material, intellectual, and spiritual possessions are the fruits of effort. They are thoughts completed, objects accomplished, visions realized.

The Vision that you glorify in your mind, the Ideal that you enthrone in your heart—this you will build your life by, this you will become.

XIII

❧

THE SEVENTH RUNG OF LIFE'S LADDER

"*I* wish to be simple, honest, natural, frank, clean in mind and clean in body, unaffected, ready to say 'I do not know,' if so be it, to meet all others on an absolute equality, to face any obstacle and meet every difficulty unafraid and unabashed.

"I wish to live without hate, whim, jealousy, envy, or fear. I wish others to live their lives, too—up to their highest, fullest, and best. To that end I pray that I may never meddle, dictate, interfere, give advice that is not wanted, nor assist when my services are not needed. If I can help people, I will do it by giving them a chance to help themselves; and if I can uplift or inspire, let it be by example, inference and suggestion, rather than by injunction and dictation. I desire to radiate life."

(The above warm and loving words were written by one of our nation's wisest philosophers, authors, and publishers in the early years of the twentieth century, Elbert Hubbard. In one drawer of Mr. Hubbard's desk he kept a collection of wise words by others and himself, not in contemplation of ever publishing them but for his own reference to help him in his daily struggles. Eventually they were published in *Elbert Hubbard's Scrap Book*. What guided and inspired Elbert Hubbard should do the same for any reader. What stimulated and uplifted him should furnish others with strength for the struggle against the eroding dullness of our workaday world. You will discover many bright stars on this rung of your ladder, stars that will enable you to deal with any darkness that lies ahead. S. P.)

Oh, unseen power that rules and controls the destinies of the children of earth, teach me the symphony of life so that my nature may be in tune with Thine.

Reveal to me the joy of being loving, self-sacrificing, and charitable.

Teach me to know and play life's game with courage, fortitude, and confidence.

Endow me with wisdom to guard my tongue and temper, and learn with patience the art of ruling my own life for its highest good, with due regard for the privacy, rights, and limitations of other lives.

Help me to strive for the highest legitimate reward of merit, ambition, and opportunity in my activities, ever ready to extend a kindly helping hand to those who need encouragement and help in the struggle.

Enable me to give a smile instead of a frown, a cheerful, kindly word instead of harshness and bitterness.

Make me sympathetic in sorrow, realizing that there are hidden woes in every life no matter how exalted.

If in life's battle I am wounded or tottering, pour into my wounds the balm of hope and imbue me with courage undaunted to arise and continue the strife.

Keep me humble in every relation of life, not unduly egotistical nor liable to the serious sin of self-depreciation.

In success, keep me meek.

In sorrow, may my soul be uplifted by the thought that if there were no shadow, there would be no sunshine.